"If Walls Could Talk"

By: Reecie Gaddy

DEDICATION

If walls could talk is dedicated to one of my biggest supporters who lost her battle but won, her war with cancer. My cousin Latoya Bradshaw. Latoya saw me through many things, but now she has her wings. That makes me want to scream toward Heaven and say Toya B. We made it happen. With a few tears and a lot of laughter I can say I have finished this chapter of my life. Toya I will continue to tell our stories while you rest in glory. Soldier, I salute you.

6/27/80-01/14/18

T, my heart is closed.

I am eagerly waiting to expose myself.

The things that I never wanted anyone to know are available for show.

Hurry, hurry and get your ticket. This shit is about to get wicked.

I have been through the thicket.

I have been a pawn in so many games.

I am surprised I remember my own damn name.

Going insane is a walk in the park for a woman that has mastered the dark.

Each time they stuck a knife in my back. They thought I would backtrack, but I moved forward.

I don't have nail scarred hands, but I have a nail scarred heart from being torn apart by the ones that claimed they loved me.

They said I was a liar, but for the lies they told God took me higher and gave me my heart's desire. Now they can witness my upcoming empire.

Yes, the whore who fed everyone who came to her door is chosen by God.

It may be hard to believe but I hope you are ready to receive this prophecy that will come forth.

ACKNOWLEDGEMENTS

First and foremost, I would like to give honor to God for impregnating me with the vision of If Walls could Talk. Giving birth to this book took many hours of labor pains. I would like to thank my mom for not aborting me and allowing the gifts in me to flourish. To my one and only blood sister, Demetrice thanks for never giving up on me when so many others did. To my daughters Shantavia, Synaria, and Aveonda thank you for allowing me to keep you up at night reading my poems. You ladies gave me such great advice. To the rest of my family and friends thank you for whatever you did good or bad. You pushed me into my destiny. To my Grandmother Overseer Margie Elizabeth Gaddy, thanks for your endless prayers. They got me through my roughest storms. To my father James E Gaddy and my grandfather Harry Gaddy, thanks for the love you gave me while you were living and the memories you left after your death. I would like to give a special thanks to Shmel Carter for allowing God to use her to help make my dream a reality. I would also like to thank my book cover designer J Ash. Dawn Divah, thank you for helping Shmel out by typing my book.

THE TRUTH

I FELL DOWN ONE TOO MANY TIMES... I
THOUGHT I WOULD LOSE MY MIND...EVERY TIME
I MADE IT TO MY KNEES... I CRIED OUT LORD
HELP ME PLEASE... EVERY TIME I MADE IT ON MY
FEET...I WAS KNOCKED BACK DOWN IN DEFEAT...
IF I HAD THE MIND SET TO JUST STAY DOWN... I
SURE AS HELL WOULDN'T BE AROUND... I HAVE
BUMP'S AND BRUISE'S BUT IM STILL HERE...I
WOULDN'T TAKE ANYTHING FOR MY JOURNEY
LET ME MAKE THAT CLEAR...IN MY VEINS RUN'S
ROYAL BLOOD... NOBODY GAVE ME SHIT I GOT IT
OUT THE MUD...I HUSTLE IN THESE STREETS
BECAUSE I HAVE NO CHOICE... I'M NOT
PERSUADED BY OTHERS I FOllOW MY OWN
VOICE...I'VE NEVER BEEN TO REHAB AND I DON'T
NEED RECOVERY... AND WHAT YOU WON'T FIND
IS MY NAME ON ANYONE'S MOTION OF
DISCOVERY...THESE DUDES OUT HERE
SNITCHING LEFT AND RIGHT... INSTEAD OF
DOING THEIR TIME THEY'D RATHER FORFEIT
THEY LIFE... I KNOW REAL OG'S SITTING BEHIND
BAR'S... BECAUSE A NO HEART ASS DUDE TRIED
TO PLAY HARD...WATCH YOUR STEP IF YOUR
COMING FOR ME...MY PEOPLE WILL PUT YOU IN
THE GROUND YO ASS TIMES THREE...YOU DO

THE MATH...THEY SAY I'M CRAZY AND I'M FINE WITH THAT...DON'T RUN UP ON ME AND YO ASS WON'T GET SMACKED...YES I TALK ABOUT GOD AND I TALK ABOUT THE STREET...WORK OUT YOUR OWN SOUL SALVATION BEFORE YOU TRY TO JUDGE ME...I PRAY TO GOD EVERY DAY AND NIGHT TRYING TO MAKE SURE MY BUSINESS IS RIGHT...I HAVE DIRT ON MY FEET AND BLOOD ON MY HANDS...BUT I'M STILL FOCUSED ON THE PROMISE LAND...MY MOM SAYS REECIE WATCH WHAT YOU SAY...WELL GOD KNOWS WHAT I'M THINKING AT THE END OF THE DAY...WHAT A MAN OR WOMAN THINK SO IS HE...GOD KNOWS MY THOUGHTS SO HYPOCRITES STOP FUCKING WITH ME...Y'ALL SAY I'M GOING TO HELL BECAUSE I CURSE... WELL LET'S POLITIC FOR A MINUTE AND YOU TELL ME WHAT'S WORSE... USING VILE LANGUAGE OR LIVING VILE...RUNNING TO THE CHURCH ACTING LIKE YOU'RE HOLY...SLEEPING WITH HALF THE CONGREGATION AND DIEING SLOWLY... PLEASE PLEASE PAY ME NO MIND...IM JUST VENTING HALF THE DAMN TIME POEM BY REECIE GADDY with Toya Bradshaw

My Life

My life isn't full of glory
My life isn't a Disney story
My life is full of drama
If you don't believe me ask my mama
My life isn't a Broadway play
I live this shit day to day
My life isn't fun and games but
I'm living life just the same
People say my life is a wreck
Well keep on talking while I come up on a check
My life isn't full of fame
But when I die they'll speak my name
My life may not have been the best
But it's my life 'til they lay me to rest

CHAPTER 1

My birth certificate say's, I was born "Blanche Dorita Gaddy" on November 21st, 1972. To the proud, I guess and very young James Ellis Gaddy and Blanche Lucille Moore. Her age at my birth was 15 and my father 17. Everything about me was unexpected including my birth. My parents were expecting a bouncing baby boy but look who came to dinner. Not only was I not a boy. I also had no name.

For those of you who don't know, black people will throw something together like they did my damn name. Both of my parents were from the deep south. My father is from a small country town called Chesterfield South Carolina, and my mom is from York South Carolina.

My parent's romance began in Boulevard Homes projects. One of the First projects built in Charlotte North Carolina. I don't know if it was Love at First sight or maybe it was lust. All I know is what I heard from other people is they couldn't keep their hands off one another. I guess the idea of being able to sleep with someone who wasn't related to you was a step up from kissing cousins.

In South Carolina a lot of people are related. The probability of you sleeping with a relative whether on purpose or accidently wasn't unheard of.

My mother and father's new-found freedom had them living carefree and careless. My parents had no choice but to grow up quickly. Even though she was young, she had made her bed, so now she had to lay in it.

My mom decided to have unprotected sex, and the result of that decision was me. My parents had no choice but to take care of me to the best of their ability. My Grandma Ella wasn't going to do it. Who could blame her? She had to raise eleven of her own children.

Sure, my Grandma Ella helped raise me. She had no problem with that. She just wasn't doing it all. Grandma Ella was born June 1st, 1920 in Chester South Carolina. Grandma Ella knew how to cook and sew extremely well. Where Grandma Ella lacked in certain areas she made up in other's. My Father had enough sense to know that living life the way it was wasn't good enough.

In 1973 my father joined the military. The U.S. Army to be exact. My parents were married that same year and we moved to Screw guard Germany. I don't have any memories of living in Germany or speaking the language. When I listen to the stories of life in Germany. They sound like bits and pieces of someone else's life but very fascinating to hear. I'm told we came back to the united states after a couple of years of being in Germany.

My mom said she was home sick. After all she was just a kid who had never been away from her parent's or sibling's. I can only imagine how my mom felt being in Germany. It was a whole different world to her. Feeling out of place would be an understatement. The only life my mom had known before moving to North Carolina was a field picking cotton with her brother's and sister's.

An old raggedy house that was held together by Love from Grandma ma Ella where she cooked on an old wooden stove and made their clothes. A hard life some would say but if you ask my mom or her sibling's they would say a simple life. When my Father had gotten my mom and I settled in Charlotte he went back to Germany.

My mom and I moved in with Grandma Ella and my Grandfather J.W. Moore who everyone called Ike. I wasn't the first grandchild to be born however I was the first grandchild to live in the home I was shipped between my mom's family and my father's. During the week I stayed with my mother's side and the weekends were spent on my father's side.

Both places were on the west side of town the only difference was Boulevard homes was the project's a public housing community. My father's parents had managed to move them out the projects and into a house. My Grandfather Harry Gaddy who everyone called "Boot" was the personal caretaker for Mr. Thomas Cadillac at the time. My grandma Margie was a stay at home mom.

Grandma Margie was a very spiritual woman. I think she had a double dose of spirituality. She's Indian and Black both races are very spiritual. My grandmother kept my cousin's and I in church all the time. When the weather was bad, and a storm came she would turn off all the light's and burn candles.

We couldn't say a word. My grandmother would say when the lord is working there must be silence. I don't know if my cousin's and I feared GOD or my Grandmother.

I enjoyed spending time with both sides of my Family. It was like I had the best of both worlds. Grandma Margie taught us about Jesus and how we're supposed to live and I'm grateful to her for that. My Grandma Ella didn't talk about the Bible, but she lived it. Sometimes when its quiet I can still hear Grandma Ella humming her old Gospel hymns that she loved to sing.

I'm not going to like to you. Having so many family member's and knowing so many family secrets can take a toll on a person. Especially a child. Before I can fully tell their stories, its only right that I start with my own. I don't know about other races, but majority of Black People have nicknames. My nickname is 'Doe Doe' and even though I answered to the name. I didn't approve of it. Doe Doe stands for a dumb bird and I'm far from that.

When I was around five years old I started kindergarten at Selwyn elementary. Selwyn had some great teacher's and the best fall festivals. Church and school played major roles in my life and friends was far and few. I had so many family member's that I didn't have a need to look outside the family for friends. However, I did have a few friend's and even more associates.

When people would see me, they would say. "Hey, aren't you one of those Moore Girls." Even though my last name was Gaddy I knew what and who they meant. Fun for me from ages 5 to 7 was making mud pies and playing hide and seek. From ages 9 to 11 fun for me had become playing in the creek, running thru the woods and playing a game called hide and get it. I was just a kid but not an ordinary kid you per say.

I Loved being around old people especially my Grandma Ella. the other thing I loved more than playing was church. I know most kids you must drag to church, but not me. I Loved music, so I always sat close to the choir. The one thing that I loved more than music was the word of God. Especially when Elder Roary preached I would get excited. I loved to listen to her, because I always learned a lot from her. I didn't do a lot of reading back then even though I could. I just trusted that what I was being taught was the truth and that my Grandmother Margie wouldn't dare have me and my cousin's listening to lies.

Even though I didn't read a lot I prayed very often. Some people probably thought that it wasn't normal for a child to pray like that. I told you that grandma Ella couldn't read but she could pray. I knew that somewhere along her life someone told her about God and Jesus. Children tend to do what they see, so I prayed.

Grandma Margie prayed in her room with the door shut. Grandma Ella Prayed anywhere and everywhere. Guess where I prayed at. I prayed everywhere and anywhere too. I was a bold child and a strong believer that God could do anything and everything. I trusted my parents to take care of me, but I knew if they didn't GOD would or, so I thought.

My Grandparent's Harry and Margie had a two-bedroom house. The weekends that I was there it would be me Winky, Niya, and sometimes Angel sleeping in the same bed. That was cool because we could play around until we fell asleep.

At least it was cool until one of my uncles started finding his way in the bed with us when everyone was sleeping. I couldn't figure out for the life of me why I was all way's the one he ended up on top of. I can still remember kicking and asking him to stop. Life for me at that point began to change. I couldn't tell anybody. My uncle would tell me if he didn't get it he would die. First, I didn't know what it was. I told him I was going to tell my grandmother, so she could help him. I wanted him to stop doing what he was doing to me and I didn't want him to die.

I stopped wanting to go to my grandmother's house on the weekends. My mom couldn't understand why. My parents had separated by then and my mom wasn't comfortable leaving me home alone. One thing about my mom was that she kept a job and she hardly ever worked on weekends. One thing for certain and two things for sure that I knew about my mother. One she was going to work. Two she was going to drink the hell out of a Budweiser like it was water. Friday's was seafood night at our house.

It never failed my mom would cook croaker fish, crab legs, coleslaw and bake beans. My mom loved music, so she would listen to her oldies, but Goodies and drink can after can of Budweiser until she was feeling herself. One night my mom was feeling so good she forgot to put water in the crab legs. She boiled them in straight Budweiser. We still ate it but in the back of my mind. I said my mom ass is going to jail. This must be some form of child abuse.

I had convinced my mom that I was old enough to stay home by myself. My mother had no reason not to trust me. I listened for the most part and I had only gotten one beating in my life. Even then it hurt my father more to do it then it did me to receive it. A few weeks had passed then the phone calls started coming...where's Dodey? Why hasn't Dorita been up here? My mom with no logical explanation said, "she'll be there this weekend." I was thinking to myself, no the Hell I won't.

I was missing my cousin's like crazy and I wasn't spending as much time with my father as I use to. I had decided to go back to my grandparent's house. I had a for sure plan at least I thought I did. I would sleep during the day and stay up during the night, so my uncle couldn't bother me. That didn't work at first. Me and my cousins would play so hard and long during the day that when night fell I could hardly keep my eye's opened. Once again Old faithful just like a dog on Top of me again. I was so glad when the summer was over I didn't know what to do with myself. I didn't have to go to my grandparent's as much and plus I was starting Middle school at Alexander Graham (AG) we called it for short.

Things had gotten a little different at home. My mom had started dating a bank robber by the name of Sam everybody called him Crow. Crow was in prison when him and my mom started dating. I hated the trips we made to the prison. It was bad enough she was going. What made it worse she dragged me right along with her. When Crow came home from prison my mom got pregnant.

My mom named my sister Demetrice, but we call her bug. I didn't need nor; did I ask for a sister. She was born 2 months before my twelfth birthday. The age difference was huge. What would we possibly have in common. I was having a hard-enough time trying to look out for myself. What could I possibly do for my sister except play with her from time to time and pray that she didn't have any pedophiles on her father's side of the family. To add insult to injury my mom moved us out of little Rock.

We moved to a neighborhood called King's park apartments, which was still on the west side of town. Not only did my mom move me away from my family in Blvd Homes. She moved me away from my associates in little Rock and closer to my father's parents. Here we go not only did I have to deal with a new man who wasn't my father, a new baby I'm a live no imitation, a new place to stay and a new school named Carmel that I had never even heard of and had no intentions on attending.

To me my world was crashing around me. Life as I had known it for 11 and a half years had changed. I was distraught, and no one gave a damn but me. I walked on egg shells in the new apartment. Crow watched me like I was in prison and he was the warden. I guess he was trying to figure me out. I didn't say much to Crow, and he didn't say much to me in the beginning. I know it had to be a difficult adjustment for crow as well. Him coming home from prison moving in with my mom, having a new baby and on top of that. He had to deal with me an 11 ½ year old girl with a grown ass woman body, and an attitude to match.

The crazy thing about the whole situation was Crow wasn't the problem he walked into an already made family with major problems already in it. The tension in my house was so thick you could cut it with a knife. The one person who I thought should have known there was a problem but didn't was my mom. I didn't hear her complain about much. Her life seems to be fine.

She had a new man, new baby and she still had me. What she didn't know was she was losing me. My mom stayed on me about getting to know Crow and giving him a chance. Truth be told getting to know Crow was the last thing on my mind. I was more concerned about uncle Albert keeping his hands off me. I wasn't disrespectful to Crow I just didn't allow him in my world. It felt like my mom was pushing him off on me. I didn't treat crow like my dad because no one could take the place of my dad no matter how sorry my dad was becoming. However, I did give Crow respect. I was taught to respect my elder's and I did just that. What I didn't do was act like everything was ok with that situation.

Not My Dad

He's not my dad he never will be
Stop pushing this man off on me

My sister is his bundle of joy
He treat's me like I'm somebody's Toy

He's your man what does that have to
Do with me

He's not my Dad can't you see

How many times do I have to say it
This is your game I don't have to play it

He's not my dad please leave me
Alone I'm still a child I'm not grown

I can't deal with this blinded Family
Shit me and this man just don't click

I know you Love him and you want
him here but I could care less
Let's make that clear

I want my own dad where is he
Somewhere running the street's when he
Needs to be with me

Ma, I Love my Dad and I don't
Know crow but I will respect him I want
You to know

Me respecting him doesn't change how I
Feel you can keep crow just give me mill

CHAPTER 2

The New Girl

It's hard enough starting a new school at the beginning. It's even worse half way through school. When I started going to Carmel. I didn't try to make friends or enemies. I joined the choir because I loved music. I joined the track team because I loved to run, and I didn't want to go straight home after school. I didn't feel like there was much there for me to do.

My mom was happy that I had gotten involved with school activities. It wasn't that she didn't want to be bothered with me. The fact that she could account for my where about when I wasn't with her gave her a peace of mind. My mom came to a lot of my track meets. She was one of my biggest supporter's. I could tell it made her proud to see me compete. My parent's thought I ran track because it was fun. Truth be told I ran because it gave me life. Running for me was like Similac for a newborn baby.

It filled me up and satisfied me all at the same time. When I ran I was free. I didn't think about being molested, my parent's separation, or if I would live to see the next day. I found out very quick that even though I wasn't trying to meet people. They were trying to meet me. Not because there was anything Extraordinary about me. The fact is that when you're an athlete or doing anything that brings attention to yourself. Whether good or bad people are going to notice.

My 8th grade year at Carmel was a lot easier than the year before. I had made a few associates and most of them was guy's. I had a couple of friend girls and even though we were close. We weren't close enough for them to know the details of my personal family life. Spring break of my 8th grade year I stayed the week at my Grandparent's house. The reason being my cousins was going to be there too. I can remember it like it was yesterday. My cousin's and I was in the bed. Winky and I was always the last two to go to sleep. Winky and I talked a lot we were close.

Winky was more like a sister to me than a cousin. Winky had fallen asleep and I was still up thinking about this boy name Marvin. Marvin was a guy who lived in Keyway and he went to my school. I was excited because he was my first real crush. The bed room was dark with a hint of light from the bathroom. I saw a shadow and I thought to myself not again. My uncle eased his way in between me and my cousin's like a snake until he was on top of me.

I closed my eyes and tears began to roll down my face. My cousin Winky started to toss and turn. My uncle must have thought she was awake because he hurried out of the room. The next day I got up bright and early. I was sitting on the front porch gazing into space.

Winky walked out and she looked at me. She said, "if you don't go and tell Grandma what our Uncle is doing to you I will." Winky was a couple of year's older than me and I looked up to her. I figured if she wasn't afraid to tell and if the consequences didn't matter to her then I would tell but I was reluctant. Winky and I walked into my grandmother's room. I began to tell my grandmother. She looked at me with disbelief and confusion. Instead of her questioning my cousin Winky. She called my aunt in the room. She was Winky and Niya's mom. My grandmother said, "have you ever seen Albert touching Doritha?"

"No mama." I looked at Winky and she looked at me. I knew the conversation was getting ready to go left.

My grandmother said, "have you gotten yourself in some trouble and trying to put in on Albert." I assumed she thought I was pregnant.

"No Grandma. I said as I stared at her.

"I just can't see him doing anything like that." My grandmother spoke as she still held a confused look on her face. Winky spoke up and told my grandma that our Uncle Albert did indeed do what I just told her he did. With two of her granddaughter's saying the same thing with no reason to lie. My grandmother said "well don't tell your father" she dropped her head and said. "He will kill him. I'll get him some help."

Well help didn't come soon enough. He did it again. I didn't tell my father because when my grandmother said he would kill my uncle the look on her face said she wasn't lying. I wasn't necessarily concerned about my uncle being dead. My main concern was my father going to prison for doing it. I decided to tell my mother. My mom said you don't have to spend the night up there anymore. Ok, I sat there, and I waited, and I waited for her to open her damn mouth and say something besides that. Since it seemed like that was all I was going to get. The conversation was over.

I walked out the door. I had a neighbor by the name of Keith Way who happened to be outside. I spoke to Keith and walked to Keyway apartments. I chilled with Marvin for a while then I went home because I had a curfew. I continued going to school every day and I acted like everything was normal. I had two friend girls that lived in King's Park. Melisa and Nicky, they were neighbor's. They were in a grade higher than me. Even though I was younger they still would conversate with me. I would go to their houses every once and a while just to talk.

In every school kids know the A listers' who's who of the big dog's. The names that stick out in my head are Anthony, Reece, Bazil, the list could go on. They were upper class man. We didn't hang out, but they knew who I was as well as I knew who they were. The guy's I hung out with was Marvin, Antonio (Nuke), Wilber and a couple more.

I didn't have to run with the Big Dog's I was a big dog in my own right. I was just on a leash.

Even though I tried to stay focused in school it was kind of hard. Some night's I would be lucky to get three hours of sleep. I would toss and turn and have awful nightmare's that woke me up sweating. My grades weren't great it was hard to study. My mind would race with thoughts of uncle Albert. I averaged a C. I guess you could say I did enough not to fail and keep my parent's off my ass. Even though Albert was my uncle other than being related by blood I had no connection to him. We didn't have conversation's or anything else. Albert was the artist of the family he could really draw. I often wondered how hand's that created such beauty could cause so much pain.

What I couldn't understand growing up and one of the things that confused me was. When you're a child they tell you to honor your mother and father and to always tell the truth, but when your truth doesn't add up with their reality they tell you to lie or be quiet. I had been quiet for year's dyeing in a personal Hell that somebody else created for me. By my grandmother telling me not to say anything to my father about the molestation. I felt like she was picking and choosing who she would save and who she would let die. She let me die daily with the reminder that I wasn't good enough to address the sexual abuse that began my fast life style. I'm grown now, and I don't have time to play the blame game. This is just an insight on what can occur in a child's life when things aren't dealt with accordingly. The thing's that I've done since I truly knew right from wrong are all on me.

Here I Am

Here I am. Can you see me?
I'm standing before you in a sea
Of regret trying to figure out
What to do next. Here I am.
Can you see me? I'm standing here with tear's
flowing from my face,
  because
I feel like such a disgrace.
Here I am. Can you see me?
I'm standing here wondering why the people
who were suppose
  to take care of me turned around and
neglected me.
Here I am. Can you see me? I'm five feet five.
With dark brown eyes with unwanted
fingerprints on my thighs.
Here I am. Can you see me?
I'm standing here using my voice, because
I have no choice. I'm speaking
for the children with silent cries.
That are covered up by lies by
people who claim they love them.
Here I am. Can you see me?
I noticed your stare.
Is it because of my hair?
Or do I have molestation written all over me?
Here I am. Can you see me?

I'm a follower of Jesus Christ and just like
him.
I've been scorned throughout my life.
Here I am. Can you see me?
I'm shy and I'm not very bold, but there's a
fire in my soul that's
burning up inside of me.
Here I am. Can you see me?
I'm very soft spoken but since GOD has
awoken the Lioness that's
with in me I no longer see mere men as
threats.
Here I am. Can you see me?
I feel like I'm on a cloud and I'm screaming
as loud as I can to get
your attention.
Here I am. Can you see me?
If I was a bolder I would just roll over all the
injustices that have
been done to me.
Here I am. Can you see me?
I came from the tribe of Judah and until
my people are free you'll continue
To hear from me.
Here I am. Can you see me?

CHAPTER 3

The one place I felt safe was at my aunt Pogal house in BHP. BHP was my comfort zone. at least it was. Aunt Pogal had a card party one night and a couple of my older cousins came with their parents. The card party lasted so long that we fell asleep. I was awakened by a tingling sensation to my vagina. To my surprise it was my older cousin performing oral sex on me. I tried to push him off me, but he held my leg's down until my body began to shake. I found out later that I was shaking because I was having an orgasm. The next morning, I couldn't even look him in his face. When they left I hoped they'd never come back. I was ashamed I was hurt and disappointed. He wasn't just my cousin he had also been my friend.

I lost my cousin and my friend all in the matter of minutes. The world seemed way too big for a 14-year-old to carry on her shoulders. My faith began to waiver. I would lay in my room on the floor on my back and say to myself GOD, where are you? Where are you? The summer before my 10th grade year I spent a lot of time at Revolution swimming pool.

Swimming was the only thing besides running and music that calmed me and kept me sain. That summer I started preparing myself for high school. I was ready physically but mentally I was fucked up. When I started South Meck I pretty much kept to myself. I decided not to try out for any activities my 10th grade year. Instead I got a job working at a restaurant called Quick's. Quick's was owned by Mr. Rob. Mr. Rob also owned a convenient store that everyone called the grapevine. Mr. Rob was the only man besides my father that validated me. When Mr. Rob gave me a job it was like he was saying I was good enough to work for a well-respected family.

I went to work every day on time and I was happy to be making my own money. I felt good about myself. South Meck High School was beginning to grow on me and my grades had gotten better. I looked forward to going to school and work. I had two coworkers that treated me nice. One was a man named Mr. Ed. Mr. Ed also worked at the famous chicken coop. The other one was a guy by the name of Fred. Fred was a senior at Myer's park High School. Fred and I saw one another all the time at work so we began to get close. Fred and I started dating and it was hard to keep us apart.

Fred would pick me up in his light blue mustang and we would hang out at his house. Even though Fred and I had a lot of sex it was more than that. Fred and I were friend's. My mom started complaining about me being with Fred so much. She forbidden me to see him. That didn't work for either of us. I tried to obey what my mom said but it was extremely hard.

Fred and I continued to date. My mom just didn't know it. I had a project to do one afternoon after school. I left my apartment headed to my friend Lay Lay's house on Barringer dr. I took a short cut thru Barringer park. When I got to the park there was a guy name Anthony there. I knew Anthony from being on West Blvd and coming into Quick's. We weren't what I would consider friend's, but he wasn't an enemy either.

Anthony asked for my number and I wouldn't give it to him because I was dating Fred and besides he was much older than me he wasn't even in school. I started to walk away when he grabbed me from behind and put his hands over my mouth and pulled me to the ground. He raped me and when he was done he said how sorry he was. He was sorry alright one of the sorriest bastards that I have ever encountered.

I grabbed my stuff and ran all the way home. When I got home my neighbor Keith Way was standing outside. Keith spoke I threw my hand up and went into the house. My mom was in the kitchen she started yelling saying I thought you had a project to do but she never came out of the kitchen. I ran up the stairs and jumped in the shower. I felt so dirty, and I wanted to wash Anthony scent off me.

I wanted to tell my mom, but I felt like if she didn't do anything about my uncle who she knew what she would possibly do about a guy she didn't know. Once again, I couldn't focus in school and I couldn't face seeing Fred at work. Fred and I broke up because I was distant, and I couldn't tell him why. I quit working at Quick's and tried to pull myself together, but it was hard. A few months went by and I started back hanging on the Blvd.

Even though I felt bad about myself I put up a front for everybody else. While hanging on the Blvd. I started seeing this guy around that everyone called Clay. Clay and I never held a real conversation we would only speak when we crossed paths. Clay reminded me a lot of the late rapper Tupac with the high Box.

I thought he was very cute, but it didn't go any further then that at first. I couldn't allow myself to think about a relationship, because I considered myself damaged goods. Damaged physically and mentally. I started to hate school. I hated to get out the bed in the morning I just wanted to sleep. I was depressed and spiraling down ward.

I needed something in my life to sustain me to make me feel whole again. My father would come and check on me from time to time, but it wasn't constant. I started to feel like after my mom left him he left me. It's something about a father's love for his daughter that's unique. It's a bond that should never be broken. It's like a chain with a missing link.

My father dated about 3 women after him and my mom separated. Sometimes it felt like he put them before me. I lost my innocence as a little girl. I lost my virginity without my permission. Now I was losing my father. There was nothing left for me to lose except my mind or my life. I was longing for something and I couldn't pin point what it was.

My mom said to my father "Reecie stay's in her room a lot lately. She doesn't talk to me much about what's going on with her. Maybe she'll open up to you."

I heard my father say, "I'll talk to her" and then he left. My father came the following weekend with what he thought was a good idea. Reecie he said "I came to get you for the weekend. I would like for you to meet my new girlfriend. We're going to stay at her house." I was excited because I would be with my father, but I wasn't thrilled at all about meeting this woman. I think every child holds out hope that their parent's will get back together after a separation or divorce and I was no different. The car ride with my dad was awkward. I wanted to breakdown and tell my father everything, but I was scared that he would be ashamed of me.

Why wouldn't he be, Hell I was. We pulled up to Westwood apartment's and my father said, "we're here." We walked into the apartment and there was an older lady standing in the Living Room. Not old like my grandmother but older then my father. My father introduced her as Miss Bailey. She seemed to be very nice, but most people are when you first meet them. She made small talk with me about school and thing's I liked to do. Then she said, "your dad told me you live in King's park with your mama."

I said, "yes Mam I do."

"My son hang's out over that way on West Blvd. you might know him."

"What's his name? I asked her.

"Brian Bailey but I call him Clay for short."

"No Mam I don't know him."

When it was time for bed she told me, I could sleep in her son's room. She told me he was not coming home or, so she thought. In the middle of the night I felt someone shaking me. I slowly opened my eyes and I heard a voice he said give me a kiss or get out my bed. To my surprise it was Brian AKA Clay. I thought to myself how ironic. To make a long story short I didn't give him a kiss and he slept on the couch.

My father started coming to pick me up on the weekends to take me to Miss Bailey's house. That's if I didn't have plans to go to my uncle Floyd and Aunt Val's house. They had three children. Even though Uncle Floyd wasn't their Biological Father we were still family. Blood couldn't make us any closer than what we already were. Especially me and Zandra.

The more time I spent at Clay's house the closer we got. We couldn't hide the attraction that we had for one another. If our parent's thought, we were about to be one big happy family they were wrong. The first time Clay kissed me was amazing. I was nervous and scared. I hadn't been with anybody since the rape. Clay wasn't rough with me and he seemed to know just what I needed to hear. We kept our relationship a secret for a few months. Clay and I would walk almost every day to meet one another. Then almost every day turned into every day.

He was like an answer to a un asked prayer. Clay came to see me at my apartment in King's Park. we talked for a while then I heard the front door open. I told Clay to get in the closet because it was my mom. My mom came up the stairs and into my room. She began to ask me about my day which seemed odd to me because she had never asked before. Then for some reason she opened my closet and there was Clay. To say she was furious was an understatement. She asked me who he was, and I told her.

My mom called my father. I couldn't begin to tell you what was said because I left. When I got home that afternoon she forbade me to see Clay again. That was hard for me because I had fallen in Love. when I did go back to Clay's house my father didn't say anything about what Clay and I had going on. He just smiled at me and said "Hey baby girl" as if nothing happened.

It wasn't long after that when my father stopped dating Clay's mom. I was at Clay's house all the time I hardly ever went home. Miss Bailey started giving me nasty look's. She would say "Clay when is this girl going home." It had gotten so bad that I was so uncomfortable even being there.

I told Clay it was over, and I went home to my mom. I didn't talk to Clay for a few day's I stopped answering his call's. I woke up one morning about four or five days of not talking to Clay and I was hurting bad and for some reason I couldn't walk. I couldn't reach the phone, so I laid in the bed and cried.

My mom and Crow was working, and I was home alone. I started to pray. Lord I don't know what's going on with my body I said but Lord I need help. Maybe about 15 minutes later I heard a knock at the front door. I started yelling. Then the knocking stopped. About 5 minutes later Clay was climbing thru my bedroom window. He had climbed up the pole to my second-floor window. I began to tell him I couldn't walk I could barely move.

Clay picked me up and took me down stairs. He called for help and I ended up in the hospital with an extremely bad kidney infection. When I got out of the hospital I went to Clay's house. I started missing a lot of day's out of school not that I was present even when I was there. Clay started being very jealous and he kept me in the house a lot. I didn't really see anything wrong with it at first. That is until I wanted to see my mom one day and he didn't want me to go. I told him I would be right back, and I headed for the door.

Clay slapped me down and pulled me back into the room. I was crying, and Clay said I'm so sorry baby I just can't stand being away from you. He began to kiss me. He slowly began to take off my clothes and then made love to me. He said "Reecie I Love you and I'll never hit you again." I wanted to be with Clay more than anything, so I forgave him. Clay had brought him a car a little white rabbit to be exact. I was happy that he had the car that meant I didn't have to stay in the house all the time.

Clay and I would go to his grandmother's house off Remount Road. She was a very sweet and intelligent woman. Clay's grandma was an Eastern Star. One night when we left his grandmother's house I was looking out the window of the car. There was a guy walking down the street. Out of nowhere Clay hit me in the face. He accused me of looking at the guy. I knew by how hard he hit me that my face was going to be messed up. When we got into the house I ran straight to the bathroom to look at my face. Sure, enough the left side of my face was swollen, and my eye was turning black. I took off my clothes and jumped in the shower.

As the water dripped off my body tears flowed down my face. Clay came into the bathroom as I was getting out the shower. He got a towel and dried me off and wiped the tears from my eyes. We walked into the bedroom and he laid me on the bed. He proceeded to have oral sex with me. Clay knew my body so well. That was the first time I felt pleasure and pain at the same time. The beatings became more frequent and the apologies stopped all together.

I don't know if his mom knew or if she even cared. She told Clay I don't know why you can't let her go she's just like her damn daddy. I didn't know what she meant by that and I really didn't care. What she failed to realize was that I wanted to leave just as bad as she wanted me to go. I guess his mom missed the memo that her son was crazier than a mother fucker. When the summer of my 10th grade year was ending I told Clay I had to go home so I could prepare for school.

He said he would take me later but when later came his plans had changed. I saw the look on his face that he was mad. I ran out the back door of the apartment and of course he followed. When Clay caught me, he beat me all in my head and face. I fell to the ground and he preceded to kick me in my stomach. I was so messed up I couldn't even get off the ground. Clay helped me up. That was the first and only time that we didn't have sex after he jumped on me. I started having real bad headaches after that.

My eyes under the bottom started getting darker from the rest of my face because of the black eye's. I cried almost every night for my father. I wanted him to come save me from this mess I had gotten myself into. My father never came. He was MIA missing in action and he wasn't even in the military anymore. In my father's defense he didn't know that Clay was beating me. I know that if he did Clay would have been dead a long time ago. I was young and confused I started mistaking lust for love.

He Beats Me

He beats me I scream for Help.
No word's will come out because my mouth
won't open.
The screams are only in my mind as the tear's
roll down my face.
I think to myself He beats me. He must hate
me.
I'm young and confused I show little emotion.
It's like I'm on a wave in the middle of the
ocean.
Every other day He throw's another blow.
Where all his anger comes from I just don't
know.
I find myself in a corner with nowhere to go.
While He kick's me repeatedly while I'm
laying on the floor.
I think to myself one day I'll be free.
It's hard to imagine this is even me.
It feels like my life is torn to shreds,
while this devious bastard is all in my head.
I'm not crazy I know I should leave, but
he has torn me down and made me believe
that no other man will ever want me.
He sits, and he laugh as he just taunts me.
One day he might kill me.
Or maybe I'll get
the draw I'll send him to meet his maker and
won't bother calling the law.

With all the Hell I've put up with Clay being dead
would be a gift.
Clay being dead wouldn't bother me at all.
I'd pick up the phone and I would just call all my,
friends he kept me from for years.
Talk about old times and shed a few tears.
Brush off the years He took from my life and
Position myself to be some king's wife.

CHAPTER 4

After the back yard beating I left the next day while Clay was gone. When I got home I was glad Keith wasn't outside I didn't want him to see my face. I knocked on the door of the apartment and my mom answered it. She looked at my face and said "Oh Hell No. he's beating on you? I told you that boy was no good for you. I can't stand his ass" she said.

Then she preceded to pick up the phone and call all my family member's. My mom wanted someone to fuck Clay up and she didn't care who did it.

Most of my guy cousins were younger than me so they couldn't do anything. The one's that were older than me were already in prison. Everyone exccpt my cousin Keith who everybody called Scrappy. He was overseas in the military. I guess GOD had everybody positioned where they needed to be. If they would have been there this story would be a lot different.

When my face cleared up I started going back to BHP. Everybody was happy to see me and glad that I was coming back around. My cousin Charlie Brown and I would sit around and talk whenever he wasn't in and out the house. I would ask him where is it that you keep going. He would just laugh and say "nowhere cuz." Something happened to me and Charlie when we were young that he or I will never forget.

Every once and a while Charlie would say "Reecie do you remember Aunt Bell?"

"You know I do. Why you always ask me that same question Charlie?" Aunt Bell was Grandma Ella's Aunt who showed up one day out of the blue when Charlie was five and I was seven. I don't remember how long she stayed. I only know she died in my grandparent's bed before she got a chance to leave.

Charlie and I didn't know she had died but the same night she died Charlie and I was upstairs in twin beds. I had my face to the wall. I heard Charlie Talking to Aunt Bell, so I turned over and it was a silhouette of her face. Aunt Bell told Charlie to be good and stay out of trouble. Charlie was a bad little boy, so I guess that's why she was telling him that. I started getting chills and I was a little scared. Charlie and I didn't know much about death really or spirits.

The next morning when we woke up Charlie asked me did I see Aunt Bell? I said no but he knew I was lying. I was still trying to figure out where the rest of her body was. When Charlie and I got down stair's he was so excited He said, "Aunt Bell was in my room last night." My Uncle Woody said, "boy stop lying Aunt Bell is dead she died last night."

"I'm not lying ask Doe Doe she saw her."

I wasn't going to say anything my uncle didn't believe Charlie and he wasn't going to believe me. My grandmother looked at me and

Charlie Not in disbelief but like she knew we wasn't lying. My grandmother didn't say a word. She smiled at us and turned to finish cooking. Charlie and I really didn't know aunt Bell but neither of us will ever forget her.

After our conversation Charlie ran out of the house again. This time I followed him. I stood on the porch while he talked to some guy in a car. I started seeing Charlie around the guy frequently, but I didn't know who he was. One day I was in BHP and Charlie was with this guy again. Charlie said Reecie, Dirt said come here. I went over to the car and we started talking. We would stop and talk every time I saw him in the neighborhood. We decided to exchange number's. Dirt's real name was Richard Herron. I preferred to call him Richard over Dirt.

Richard called me one day and asked if I wanted to go with him. I said yeah, I wasn't doing anything anyway. Richard and I went and got a room. We chilled and talked, and I told him about Clay and all the I had been going through. Richard listened he was understanding, and he didn't judge me. While I talked, Richard looked at me like he could see right through me. Not who I was at that moment but who I could be.

One thing led to another and we had sex. When Richard came inside of me I felt sick as a dog suddenly. I couldn't figure out what was wrong with me. I would still see Richard in the neighborhood and we would talk. He didn't treat me any different. Richard would ask me if I needed any money and at first, I wasn't used to a man giving me anything except an ass whooping. Richard had a friend name Garnett that lived in my neighborhood with his girlfriend. I would stop by and talk to them after school sometimes.

Weeks went by and I started throwing up and sleeping a lot. I went to Garnett's apt and I told his girlfriend that I thought I had a virus. She was about 5 or 6 years older than me, so I figured she knew what I could take to feel better. She said have you taken a pregnancy test. I said no I'm not pregnant. I hadn't been sleeping with Clay and I had only slept with Richard one time. I couldn't possibly be pregnant by Richard. Clay and I had been having un protected sex for over a year and he never got me pregnant.

You can tell by my state of mind that I was young and immature. Even though I was sixteen I didn't know you could get pregnant on the first time. Garnett's girlfriend went and got me a pregnancy test and sure enough I was pregnant. She said when are you going to tell Richard? I told her I wasn't going to tell him anything. Richard was the last person I was concerned about telling.

I didn't want to tell my mother and most definitely not my Dad. I thought for day's about how I would tell them. It was hard for me and I asked GOD for strength and guidance. Even though I asked GOD for help I didn't wait for him to answer. I ran away from home. I had always been better at writing what I had to say or saying nothing at all. If I would have wrote back, then like I do now I would have written my parent's a poem. My

mom's poem from my sixteen-year-old mind set
would have went like this.

I'm Pregnant Ma

I'm pregnant ma
I'm not trying to put all this on you but we
Never talked about sex and I didn't know
What to do
I know I broke all the rules, but I promise
You ma I'm gonna finish school
It's hard to tell you but I can't tell my Dad
It's going to break his heart and make him sad
Ma, I don't know anything about a baby
except
How to feed them and change them maybe
I wish I could take all this back when life
Was much simpler and I still ran track
They say babies are a gift from God and even
Though I believe it it's still kind of hard
Ma, I know a baby wasn't in our plans but
The greatest gift's come from the master's
hands.

My poem to my father would have been a
difficult one to write. By my father being ex-military
and very disciplined with high expectations of me
would make me choose my words carefully but still
get to the point. My father's poem would have gone
like this.

Daddy I'm Pregnant

Daddy I'm pregnant
I know you had big dreams for me but'
I'm going to make it you wait and see
Daddy I know I let you down but when
I needed you most you weren't around
Daddy you never talked to me about boy's
I guess you thought I would stay little and
always play with toys
Daddy I know it's hard to believe it was
A shock for even me
Daddy I don't want you to be bitter if
You want me to abort it I will consider
Daddy it's me I'm on my knee's I need you
To forgive me daddy please
Daddy if GOD can forgive you for all you've
done can you forgive
me for just this one
Daddy if you turn your back on me that
Would be Hard but if I don't have you I still
have GOD

CHAPTER 5

When I left home I stayed with different associates for days. I ran into one of my child hood friends by the name of Mushy while I was away from home. Mushy convinced me to go with her to her aunt's house in the university area. I didn't know where I was at first the only side of town I knew anything about was the westside. The university area was nice, but I was out of my comfort zone.

I was gone for about a month when I decided to call my aunt Pogal. When the phone began to ring I started to hang up, but I couldn't. When I heard aunt Pogal's voice I was silent. I just held the phone. She said hello a few times and then she said, "Doe Doe is that you?"

"Yes, Mam it's me."

"Thank you, GOD." I could hear the relief in her voice as she continued to ask me questions. "Where are you? Are you ok? Why did you leave?" Tear's began to roll down my face and my voice began to crack.

I said, "Aunt Po I'm pregnant." She tried to comfort me as much as she could over the phone.

"It's okay baby just come back home. Your parents are worried to death about you." I agreed to go home but I didn't go that same day. I had meet a nice family by the name of Knuckles. Mr. and Mrs. Knuckles had three sons'. Their son Taylor and I became friend's and about three days after I talked to aunt Pogal, Taylor and his father gave me a ride home.

When I walked into the apartment the only hug I received was from my five-year-old little sister. That wasn't surprising to me because I don't recall either of my parent's hugging me when I was growing up or even saying they loved me. Even though they never said it I knew that they loved me. I knew my mom was happy I was home even though she never said it.

What she did say was "Reecie, when did you start hanging out with drug dealer's?"

I said "drug dealer's? I don't know any drug dealer's ma."

My mom said, "from what I'm told your pregnant by one of the biggest drug dealers' in the city."

"Ma, I don't know where you're getting your information from, but some body miss informed you."

"Charlie Brown told us. He's working for him." I thought to myself what the hell is next? I'm pregnant and Charlie's a damn drug dealer, thing's couldn't get any worse. Then I found out Richard had a girlfriend.

I started avoiding Richard's phone call's not because he had a girlfriend. I didn't want to talk about the pregnancy. I wanted it all to go away. Richard being a drug dealer was a game changer. I didn't know how to talk to a drug dealer it was cool when I thought he was a regular guy. I had no idea what kind of drug's he sold the only drug I had ever heard of was weed but I had never seen any.

The next couple of weeks was crazy in the house. My mama was walking through the house talking shit. She said Richard probably had an ass load of baby's already with different baby mama's. My mom said to me "I hope those karate lessons I paid for pay off because you're going to have to fight. Oh, and another thing your father will be here later to talk to you."

I mumbled under my breath he might be here, but I won't be. I left and caught the bus to BHP. when I got to BHP instead of going in aunt Pogal's house I sat on the curb near her apartment. While I was sitting there my mind went back to my childhood. I thought about my grandfather Harry and how he would pick my grandmother, me, Winky and Nicky up from church.

Every time we got to my cousin's neighborhood in Greenville we would slide down in the back seat of the car, so the boys wouldn't see us in our grandfather's Black 1964 Cadillac. We didn't know anything about car's it was so long, and we were embarrassed. We didn't know that Cadillac's were good car's and just about anybody that didn't have one wanted one.

I thought about my trips to chesterfield South Carolina with my father. I thought about how my dad taught me to fish, cut the head's off and gut them. And even though my dad didn't say much when we were together just being with him meant the world to me. And to hear him say baby girl meant he was acknowledging me.

While I was thinking back on Yester year's a car came by and slammed on break's, that snapped me back into reality. It was Richard. He smiled at me and said I know your pregnant. I didn't know what to say to him I was still a little shy, so I dropped my head and he drove off. I went home as late as I could, so I would miss my father but when I walked through the door he was sitting in the living room.

He looked at me and said, "Hey baby girl is you ok?"

I said, "yes sir I'm fine." My father didn't ask me anything other than that. Then the house phone rang my dad went to answer the phone and my mom yelled don't answer my damn phone. My dad answered any way and said you paid your dime speak your damn mind.

My mom was too pissed off and my dad just laughed and said "Blanche it's just Pogal it's not Crow. She's checking to see if Reecie made it home." My dad stayed for about thirty more minutes and then he left.

The next day I signed up for Tap's a school for pregnant girl's the day school started Clay came by the house. He said Reecie I know your pregnant. Clay said can I give you a ride to school, so we can talk I promise I won't put my hands on you. I agreed, and Clay opened the car door for me and I got in. Clay and I talked, and he told me how much he missed me, and the crazy thing was I missed certain things about him too. Clay was the second real relationship I had, and I wanted him to change so we could be together.

I considered Clay's good quality's and found reason's on why I should get back with him and I over looked the bad things about him and the reason's I shouldn't get back with him. Clay and I started back dating I was around four months pregnant. I finally spoke with Richard and we talked about the baby and I told him I went back to Clay.

Richard was concerned not because he wanted to be in a relationship with me. He was concerned because he knew Clay had been abusive in the past. He was concerned because I was pregnant with his first and only Biological child. My mom was wrong he didn't have an ass load of kids with different baby mama's. I was messing around with my mom and I said I guess we'll never know if I benefited from those karate classes'.

My mom was mad as hell she said don't play with me Reecie. My mom couldn't stand Richard and she didn't even know him hell I barely knew him myself. The fact that he was a drug dealer was all she needed to know. I started having cravings for Chinese food from a place near my house. Just about every day I ate shrimp fried rice and chicken wing's which Richard paid for.

Richard would send his cousin Bruno or one of his workers to bring the food because he didn't want a confrontation with my mom. Bruno was the one that came the most. Bruno said to me I will be happy as hell when you have this baby, so you can stop feeding my little cousin cat's. I said if it's cat it's the best cat I ever tasted, and we laughed. Clay and I were doing good and he didn't put his hands on me anymore, but he was still jealous.

I couldn't go anywhere without him except school and the bathroom. He however went were ever he wanted while I was stuck in the house. Clay went to all my Doctors' appointments and he made sure I was ok. The pregnancy had me sick as a dog I literally thought I was going to die. If I wasn't throwing up I was sleeping. The day's I could make it to school I didn't accomplish much. I was either sleep on my desk or in the bathroom throwing up what seemed to be my insides.

Eventually I stopped going to school all together. I didn't see my father, nor did I speak with him during the duration of my pregnancy. My father's dream of me going into the military like he did had gone down the drain and so had my self-esteem. Clay's mom was even worse after I got pregnant. She would say "why are you so in love with this damn girl? She's pregnant and it's not even your baby. Eventually she'll leave you like her daddy did me."

Clay said, "she's nothing like her father and besides you ran her dad away." Truth be told Clay and me being together helped my father make the decision for my father to leave Ms. Bailey. The last five months of my pregnancy was depressing. I wasn't around Winky, Zandra or any of my family that meant the most to me. When I was nine months' pregnant I decided to go to aunt Pogal's house in BHP.

I didn't tell Clay I was leaving because he wasn't home. I felt like I was losing my mind the walls were closing in on me in that apartment. When I got off the city bus I saw Tyvonne sitting on the porch. Tyvonne said "hey Doe Doe how you are doing?"

I told Ty I was fine.

"When is the baby coming?" She wanted to know.

I said, "soon Ty soon." I walked into the house as I started down the hall way my water broke. I screamed and Aunt Pogal and Uncle Mickey ran out of the kitchen where they had been playing cards. I walked back to the porch by Ty and waited on the ambulance. The contractions and the pressure seemed too much for a young teenager to endure. As much as I wanted the baby to be healthy I didn't won't to die delivering her.

I said GOD I know I don't have any right to ask you anything after what I've done but father please let my baby be ok and let me live to tell about it. Another thing GOD the contraction's and pain is so bad it's cutting off my breath just as I was saying that a nurse came in and said your about seven centimeters and we can give you an epidural that should help with the contractions. I said Thank you GOD. I gave birth to a seven-pound two-ounce little girl who Richard named Shantavia Tawanna Gaddy.

Richard wasn't at the hospital when I gave birth, but Clay was. When it came to sign the birth certificate I didn't allow anyone to sign it. Richard would have been there, but I didn't let him know when I went in labor and that was my fault. I was more concerned about what Clay would think and how he felt that I cheated Richard out of his right to see his daughter being born.

When the time came for my daughter and I to leave the hospital I had a setback. I couldn't leave but Shantavia could. My mom left with Shantavia and took her straight to BHP to aunt Pogal's house. My mom said before she could get out of the car good a lady ran out of an apartment across from my aunt Pogal's. She said can I show my cousin his daughter. My mom said she was reluctant, but she followed and when she got inside the apartment she saw an old friend girl name Charlene who she hadn't seen for years. Charlene looked at Shantavia and said she's my son's baby for sure.

Then my mom said Richard came out the room. She said he didn't say a word. He picked the baby up and took her in the room and closed the door. My mom said it seemed like they were in there for hours. Richard came out the room and asked my mother where I was. My mom said she began to tell him. He asked her what the baby needed. She began to tell him, and he went straight and bought it. My mom began to like Richard because he was real respectful, and he showed her that he was going to be there and take care of his child.

When I was released from the hospital after a week I stepped into mommy mode. Late night feeding's and changing, crying till the sun came up with no relief in sight. She would be dry and fed and she still hollered at the top of her lung's I couldn't take it. It seemed like this baby was draining the life out of me. When she was sleep I couldn't help but see how beautiful and perfect she was. When night came it was a different story I would start crying as soon as she started crying. My mom began to come and get the baby during the night, so I could get some rest.

When Shantavia was about two months' old I went back to Clay's house. My cousin Winky started coming to get Shantavia on the day's she was off and take her to see my father and grandmother. Winky was a real-life saver when it came to give me break's with Shantavia it felt like she knew exactly when to show up. I began to feel bad because I didn't have a plan for my life or my baby's life. I wasn't prepared, and my life wasn't going anywhere and by the looks of it Clays wasn't either.

Clay may have been comfortable staying home with his mother, but I wasn't. When Shantavia turned eight months I decided to go to job corps'. I told my mom three days before I was leaving that I had joined. I told her I was going to Batesville Mississippi, without a dime in my pocket.

When I got to the bus station and began loading the bus I could see my mom standing there with Shantavia in her arms with tears flowing from her face. I could see the pain in my mother's eye's, but I couldn't turn back. It was like I was leaving a bad dream behind and awaiting me was a brand-new life. When the bus left the station, it was like a weight lifted off me. Selfish some would say, and I'm inclined to agree but I didn't know what else to do.

I felt like my mother would be a better person to raise her because she was so good with my sister. I didn't think about the strain it would put on her life or the changes she would have to make. My mom didn't have to take care of her financially because Richard did that. When I got to Batesville I started working on my Ged and I started taking welding classes.

I wanted to be an underwater welder because they made good money. If everything went how I planned it, I would have been able to take care of my daughter on my own. The only thing that disturbed me when I got to job corps was that they had gang's, real life gang's. There were Gangster Disciples, Blood's and Crips not like the gangs from Charlotte the He Men and G men shit got real when I left the city.

I made a few friends and one of them was an Indian. We had the smart idea to tattoo ourselves with a needle and ink. Then we stuck our fingers and when blood came out we rubbed our fingers together and called one another blood sisters and brothers. As you can see even though I had a baby I was still young minded. I would call home to speak with my mother and check on my daughter.

Each time I talked to Shantavia I could hear her clearer and clearer. I started feeling bad because I left my mom high and dry. I felt like the scum of the earth. I didn't have a connection with GOD like I use to I had a baby that I couldn't afford to take care of I was depressed my self-esteem was low damn near gone I had no money I had let not just my parent's down but the whole family. I had self-hatred and I was sick and tired of people saying you're going to get it together you're a beautiful person inside and out. I had so much self-hatred and nobody knew it but me. I left the one true love of my life who was connected to me more than myself to be raised by someone else. I thought I was doing what was best for her but in all actuality, I did what was best for me. I wasn't strong enough or women enough truth be told I wasn't a woman I was just a girl.

Best for You

I thought I was doing what was best for you.
Sadly, I found out that wasn't true.
I thought I was grown and set out to
began a life of my own.
I left you behind and in the back of
my mind I was giving you a better life.
But how could your life be better without
me?
I carried you 9 months and endured the pain.
Now I must endure the shame of leaving you
behind.
I let people say what they wanted and think
what they must.
While I continued my journey and continued
to trust GOD to prevail.
I asked GOD to forgive me and not have me
a reserved spot
into hell.
I prayed every day that you defined your way
and the Angels would
guide you along your path, and occasionally,
make you laugh.
I prayed that us being apart wouldn't put a
strain on your little heart
and we'd be together soon someday.

To Shantay
Love Mama Reecie

CHAPTER 6

I had been in Mississippi for about three months and everything was going good except the fact I was missing my daughter. My Ged classes were going well, and I was loving the welding classes that I was taken. One afternoon after class I went back to my dorm and there was a group of girls waiting on me. They accused me of stealing hair Jam.

One of them hit me and I found out that day my karate classes paid off. They didn't bother me again, but I got kicked out of Job Corp for fighting. I was devastated on the ride back home because I had no idea what I was going to do. Charlotte for me was like a trap I couldn't win being in that city even though it was my city.

Everybody was happy to see me especially my daughter. I thought she had forgotten about me. Somehow Clay found out I was home, and he started coming around. I wasn't interested in any type of relationship at that point in my life I just needed guidance. I still hadn't seen my father I had no idea where he was. He didn't come look for me and I didn't look for him either. Truth be told when I needed my dad the most he was nowhere to be found.

I was home for about five months when my home girl Tara introduced me to her cousin Latrell. Latrell was about six and a half feet tall with a Carmel complexion and good hair, the brother was fine. We all started hanging out and we had some good times together. Tara said you know Latrell likes you right. I said no, why would he? I was an average looking female with a baby and low self - esteem.

I couldn't understand why a guy that was fine as he was would want me. When he would try and hold my hand I would pull away at first because I was shy. I would laugh, and he would say what's so funny? I didn't have an answer I really didn't know why I

was laughing. Latrell and I started hanging out without Tara and our friendship started being sexual hook up's almost every day. We still had fun in between laughing and playing around. That is until I found out I was pregnant again.

Shantavia was only one and a half year's old and I was only nineteen. I told Latrell as soon as I found out and he didn't have a problem with it. At least he said he didn't. A lot of people that I knew started telling me he was denying the baby behind my back. He never once said anything to me about it, but he stopped coming around.

It was like he was a ghost that vanished in thin air. The only person I knew to call that wouldn't judge me was Richard. I was crying, and I told Richard that I was pregnant, and Latrell was denying the baby.

I told him my life was over and I was going to give the baby up for adoption. Richard said no, you're not. Richard said every baby needs a father and I will step up and help you raise the baby. I had to meet Richard one day in BHP to get some money. Richard came to the car. In one hand he had the money in another hand he had a large paper bag. He said which one do you want? Me with my curious self- reached for the bag.

It had big white block's I didn't know what it was, so I gave it back and took the money. I found out later it was cocaine. About six months later Richard was set up and he received fifteen year's federal time. Shantavia was two years old at the time. My mom decided to move us to Providence Rd. When we moved there I got two jobs to take care of my kids one at Mc Donald's and the other one was at Rack room shoe's.

One day while I was working at McDonalds Clay showed up at my job and pulled out a gun on me. When another coworker came from the back he ran off. When my shift was over I began to walk through a path to get home.

Half way thru the path I looked back, and Clay was sprinting behind me. I was scared, and I didn't know what to do so I started to run. Clay yelled stop, or I will shoot you in the back and just when he said that a lady driving a van came thru the bushes and picked me up.

She came out of nowhere and I was grateful. I like to think she was my guardian angel. She gave me a ride home and I was scared to go in. I had one of my neighbors check the apartment. He said everything was clear. Shortly after that my mom and Crow came home they had my little sister and Tyvonne with them.

Me and my mom Tyvonne and my sister were sitting on my twin beds talking about what happened. Out of nowhere my mom yelled Clay's under the bed. Crow came out of the other room and beat the hell out of Clay. If they didn't think Clay was crazy before they knew he was crazy, then.

I felt bad for Clay for some reason and I continued to talk to him on the phone. A few weeks later I went to see clay and I took Shantavia with me. When I got ready to leave I couldn't find my wallet. I had Shantavia in my arms when Clay found my wallet and threw it at me.

The wallet hit Shantavia in her face and ripped flesh from the corner of her right eye. I was furious. I was mad at Clay but more so myself for allowing it to happen. Never in my wildest dreams did I think that a decision that I made would have gotten my daughter hurt.

Shantavia had to be hospitalized for over a week. While she was their Alonzo Mourning came to visit the kid's and he sat with me and Shantavia for a while. Alonzo Mourning was very nice and down to earth. Even though he played in the NBA with the Charlotte Hornets at the time he didn't treat us like we were beneath him. I just hate that it took something tragic to happen to my daughter to be in the presence of a great man. That was the straw that broke the camel's back Clay and I were finished.

Were Done

To hurt me is one thing but to hurt my child is another

I know I have forgiven you in the past but not this time brother.

I do love you, but I love my daughter more and there's no

way in hell I can keep this behind a closed door.

I must tell her father because he deserves to know.

Not to tell him would be trifling and that trifling shit would show.

I know you said you were sorry and sorry you sure are but sorry

doesn't change the fact that you went too damn far.

God says I must forgive you, so I don't have a choice.

I must speak for my daughter because she doesn't have a voice.

My daughter's pain is my problem and I am the reason she's hurt.

I should have left instead of waiting for this relationship to work.

I don't care how lonely or depressed I may get I put that on my daughter

this is it.

I won't shed tears over this mess it being over is only for the

best.

My mom told me you were bad news and to leave you alone,

but I didn't listen because I thought she was wrong.

She said a hard head makes a soft ass I should have listened to every word

She said,

but I chose to disobey her and continually bumped my head.

CHAPTER 7

While staying with my mother I felt like me and my kid's being there put a strain on her even though she never said it. I decided to put in applications for public housing. The waiting list were six months to a year-long.

While I was waiting I tried the school thing again but not a traditional school I went to Harding night school. I was determined to finish school not only for myself but mostly for my mom. As far as my dad was concerned I started to care less about whether he was disappointed in me, because I was disappointed and let down by him.

My respect for my dad didn't turn to disrespect it turned to disbelief. I still had a hard time understanding how a man who played a major role in his child's life could fail her when his marriage failed. My father didn't even know that I went back to school because he was nowhere to be found.

While I was in night school I met a guy named Winston from New York. Winston sat behind me in class. Winston was a couple of years younger than me and for some reason he found it amusing to throw spitballs at the back of my head. He was aggravating as hell.

One day while I was at Aunt Pogal's house in BHP my cousin Buster walked in the apartment and when he walked in so did Winston. He approached me like he and I were friends. He said what's up? I said nothing will ever be up if you keep acting like a child and throwing spitballs at me.

Winston apologized, and he and I began hanging out without Buster. He was always joking and playing around, and little did I know I needed that. Laughter and fun was a thing of my past along with my childhood. I had two kids depending on me and with Richard being gone I had no time to play.

About four months into night school my mom got a second job and I had to quit night school. A few months later I received a letter from Charlotte Housing Authority. They offered me an apartment in South Side Homes. I was beyond excited.

When my mom came home I told her about the letter and she wasn't pleased at all. My mom said you don't have to leave those apartments are rough. I thought to myself they can give me a tent I'm out of here. Besides my mom and aunts would tell me and my cousins if you want to be grown and do grown people stuff get your own shit.

I didn't really want to be grown but by me having two kids I had to hurry up and act grown. Winston and I continued to see each other and when I moved into my apartment he came with me. I wasn't in my apartment a week when I started receiving phone calls from Clay. Clay asked me about Winston. He said if I can't have you no one will.

Maybe an hour later Winston and I went upstairs and as soon as we entered the bedroom shots were fired and bullets entered the apartment and we both fell to the floor. I called the police and when they got there my phone rang it was Clay. He asked me if that nigga was still there? "If he is I'm on my way back and this time I won't miss."

While Clay was talking crazy, I gave the phone to the police. I don't know why I did that he cursed the police out too. I knew for sure that Winston and I were done. I told him that I understood if he no longer wanted to date me. To my surprise he said I love you and I'm not leaving and he stayed.

That incident brought us even closer than we were before. Clay ended up getting locked up and he went to prison for shooting in an occupied dwelling. He never bothered me again after that.

Shantavia didn't like being in South Side because they did a lot of shooting at night. She was terrified. I spoke with my mom and she and I agreed that Shantavia would be better off with her and Synaria would stay with me because nothing seemed to bother her.

Shantavia came to South Side on the weekends and during the summer. Winston didn't have any children at the time, but he was great with my kids. Dating Winston was a lot different from being with Clay. I had freedom with Winston and a peace of mind.

The only problem that Winston and I seemed to have was money. By neither one of us finishing school it was hard for us to get jobs. I was getting extremely frustrated and unsure of how I would take care of my kids. Even though I was receiving welfare I was uncomfortable doing so. I felt very unproductive and I complained to my mom about welfare and the system because I was embarrassed. My mom got tired of hearing it and she said to me "Reecie your father is a vet and on top of that both of us work. The taxes that the government takes out of our checks help fund these programs." I felt better after talking to my mom however it didn't change the fact that welfare wasn't enough to take care of my kids. Facing the dilemma of my money issues I decided to go to a Jamaican club that I enjoyed having a drink and clear my mind.

While I was there I met a guy by the name of Zeb. Zeb and I talked over drinks and he said he was an investment banker. I didn't know much about that, but I did know that it involved money. Zeb and I met a few more times at the club and he said I know how you can make some money. I said how? Zeb said I can show you better than I can tell you give me your address. I said hold the hell up I don't sale my body and I have a boyfriend.

Zeb said no, no, no that's not what I meant. I decided to give him my address. I told Winston about Zeb and that he would be coming by. A few days later Zeb showed up and we sat at my kitchen table. To my surprise Zeb pulled out blocks that looked exactly like the ones Richard had three years before.

The only difference was the color, his was a darker white. I said so you're an investment Banker and a cocaine dealer. He laughed and said no Reecie. I'm not an investment banker at all. I said why did you lie? He said how many drug dealers do you know that advertise to people they don't know what they do for a living.

After saying that he said look closely Reecie and he pulled out a razor blade. He preceded to cut off the block first small pieces. He said this is a dime, this is a twenty, and this is a fifty. He said these are what your users normally buy. They may even ask you for a half of eight which is seventy- five dollars.

Then he said if you're going to sell weight to other dealers that's a whole different ballgame. He said this is an eight ball it's one hundred and fifty. A quarter is three hundred and a half of ounce is six hundred dollars. An ounce is a thousand dollars.

Zeb said if they want more than that they are going to have to go through me. Then he pulled out a scale and showed me what the weight should be for each one. I said how am I supposed to know if it's any good.

"Reecie the dope is good." Zeb said but if it would make you feel better you can get someone to test it out. I said okay, and I called my aunt Mae and she came over. My aunt came in and saw all that dope she thought she was in cocaine heaven. She took a hit and she got quiet then her mouth started twitching and she said it's good it's good.

It didn't take long for the word to get out that I was in business. Aunt Mae, Aunt Helen and Aunt Katherine started bringing their associates to me. The money started coming in fast and plenty of it. I was able to buy my daughter's name brand clothes and shoes. I was also put in a position to help take care of a few of my cousins.

It felt good to be able to give my mom money and anyone else in my family that needed it. A few of the guys in the neighborhood would come and ask me for a double up. I said what's a double up? Zeb didn't say anything about double ups. A double up is when someone gives you less than what a half of eight cost so eventually they will make enough to buy the whole thing.

For example, if they give you thirty- five dollars you give them enough to make seventy or eighty dollars off it. I did that occasionally, but not too often because you lose money doing that. Keep in mind things have changed since then that was in the late nineties.

My decision to move to South Side put me on a completely different side of town then my mom and little sister. Even though I was further away from my mom I was in walking distance to my Aunt Katherine who lived in Wilmore with my little cousins John and Arbary. My aunt Helen was also in walking distance. My Aunt Helen was dating a drug dealer by the name of Truesdale who lived on Bank Street.

Katherine and Helen are my mom's two youngest sisters, and both was addicted to cocaine at the time. My aunt Helen had three kids Tamika, Travis, and Johnesha. With me selling drugs and being so close, the drugs they didn't get from Truesdale they got from me for free.

Even though I didn't want to give my aunts drugs, what I didn't want even more then that was them having to do something crazy to get it from one of the dudes on the block. Besides my aunts was doing drugs long before I started selling the shit. It didn't make it any better that I gave it to them, but it made common sense to me that I would be the one to support their habit from time to time. They were family we had the same blood flowing through our bodies and I loved them.

The guys on the block didn't give a damn about them and I couldn't let the guys have my aunts turning tricks to get crack. I thought about my little cousins and I didn't want people messing with their minds about what their parents did in the streets for drugs. I can't say that I wish I wouldn't have moved to South Side and got caught up in the drug game. My failures, my good and bad decisions, and my struggles have made me who I am today, a survivor.

My mom didn't approve of me selling drug's but there wasn't much she could do about it. I was in my own place and besides she was dating a drug dealer at the time by the name of Henry. During this time my sister was in middle school at Carmel where she was a cheerleader.

Even though my mom had a decent job cooking at Presbyterian hospital now known as Novant health it didn't allow her the money to buy a lot of name brand clothes or hundred-dollar tennis shoes. However, my drug money allowed me to buy Jordan's not only for my kids but also my sister. My mom kept my little sister clean and dedicated a hundred and ten percent to my sister and her future.

Winston didn't get into the game he just hung around and smoked weed all day. Winston stayed high and he kept me laughing. Everything was going good until Winston's routine started to change. One day I was looking in the bottom of my closet and I found a mask and a big bag of change. I asked Winston what was going on and he said nothing. He took the mask and change out of the apartment a couple of weeks later.

Winston didn't show up at the house. I found out he was messing around with my cousin Charlie's baby mama. I was hurt, and I felt betrayed. I went to BHP ready to fight not her but him. I was in a relationship with him not her she owed me nothing. My aunt Dot came and grabbed me I was crying, and she began to tell me he wasn't worth it. After I calmed down I went home and feel apart.

I took about twenty- five to thirty pills because I felt like I wanted to die. I don't remember who called the paramedics, but I ended up at the hospital getting my stomach pumped. I was in the hospital for a few days and then they transferred me to mental health because of the suicide attempt.

I realized I really didn't want to die I was crying out for help. I didn't realize what a major part of my past was playing in my life. I realized that I wasn't so in love with Winston that I couldn't live without him. I had abandonment issues that started with my Dad. When I went back home my friend Freda came by. She started telling me how stupid I was and all this other crap I didn't want to hear. I knew that she was on the outside looking in and she had no clue what the hell she was talking about.

I was so grateful to GOD that I didn't die. I started back hustling right away because even though Winston was gone my kids was not. Whatever Winston had going on with Barbara didn't last long. A few weeks went by and he was at my house asking me to forgive him. I forgave him because he had never put his hands on me and everyone deserves a second chance.

Everything was going good until the police showed up and arrested Winston for robbing restaurants and putting people in the freezer. I found out that day that hustling wasn't in Winston's blood, but robbing was. I missed Winston and there wasn't anything I could do. I didn't feel bad about him going to prison because even though I sold drugs I didn't believe it was ok to strong arm hard working people. That chapter of my life with Winston was over but my life of selling drugs wasn't.

After Winston was gone my mentality toward men was horrible. I slept with who I wanted to when I wanted to, and I made no apologies for doing it. This unapologetic sex was pleasing to my flesh, but I didn't know it was killing my spirit. I treated men like they treated me like I was replaceable. I didn't need their money, because I had my own. I also had my own car, so I didn't need a ride. Being that my kids had a lot of my time I didn't even need companionship. I wasn't looking for love so what else could they offer me other than sex.

There wasn't one person during that time that cared about my spiritual well-being. Nobody ever asked me to go to Church with them or even offered up a word of prayer. There was not any mention of Christ. The more I was out of the will of God the easier it became to do Godless things. If this book help one girl or boy, woman or man to be a better person then that is fine with me. I pray that it will help someone from getting caught up in sexual sin that will drain the very life out of them after it has served its purpose.

I wish someone would have explained this to me at a young age. My body is the temple of God that is to be presented as a living sacrifice. Holy and pleasing to God. Romans 12 and 1. Having lack of knowledge I found myself engaged in sexual immortality that has proven to have a strong hold on me. keep in mind my body had been trained in sexual perversion since I was a child. Once you have been trained or introduced to something that controls majority of your life either mentally, physically, or spiritually it is hard to change the mindset.

When He Left Me

When he left me, I felt like I wanted to die but after
a failed suicide attempt I
   realized I had been living a lie.
   I thought I needed him like I needed a crutch I found
out the attachment I
   had to him was way too much.
   I gave him more of me then I gave myself. I thought
if I had him I didn't
   need anyone else. I guess hustling made me blind.
   I didn't even notice he was no longer mine.
   When the smoke settled, and the shit hit the fan I
realized I didn't truly
   know this man. It's funny now and I laugh at myself
while I was focused on
   my money he was screwing somebody else.
   I guess that goes to show it doesn't matter how
much money you have if
   someone is unhappy they'll choose another path.

CHAPTER 8

Family Business

I wasn't the only young female in my family that hustled. My cousin Zandra and I hadn't seen one another in a minute and when we hooked back up it was like old times except we both sold drugs. When we were younger being drug dealers never crossed our minds. With our parents being GOD loving hard working people there was no way anybody could have predicted our life of crime.

Zandra had always been over protective of me and by me being quiet and laid back and her being loud and outgoing with her tendency to get into fights and even start one was a big difference between us.

I never liked trouble I always avoided it by any means necessary. Zandra didn't look for trouble but she didn't know how to avoid it if it came her way either. Zandra and I started hanging out at my apartment and when I ran out of drugs or just didn't want to sell any she took over. It was a win, win situation for me because both of us were single parents trying to raise our kids.

Neither one of us thought about what it was doing to the people or their families that we sold drugs to. Selling drugs became the norm for me, it was like walking in the park on a sunny afternoon without a care in the world. With Winston being gone and me with extra time on my hands I started going out with Zandra and her sister.

Zandra had started seeing this guy and he had a friend. Zandra wanted me to meet him. She said he thinks he's GOD's gift to women. Zandra told him I have the perfect person for you. Zandra knew I had a I don't give a damn about a man attitude. If it worked out it worked out and if it didn't fuck it.

When Olando and I met I thought he was handsome with a college boy preppy look. That was new for me I was used to straight up gangster dudes. Olando and I started seeing each other on a regular. I guess we were dating without discussing that we were dating.

Olando lived alone in a house his mother owned so that gave me somewhere to go besides the hood. Being at Olando house gave me a break from hustling. With me being up all day with my daughter Synaria and then hustling all night had me extremely tired.

Olando didn't like the fact that I sold drugs but his feelings for me was much stronger than his dislike of my life style. Olando was a security guard at the time and he didn't do anything to break the law.

Olando stayed on me about me selling drugs and I tried my best to stop. Even though I cared very much for Olando my addiction to fast money and fast cars out weighed my feelings for a good man. I had been so used to taking care of myself that I didn't know how to let a man come into my life and be a man.

I pulled away from Olando and in return he slept with my cousin's friend Melony. That was a mistake. Olando called me saying Melony was walking up and down his street with a gun because he didn't want to deal with her. I don't know why he called me I could have cared less about what he and Melony had going on. I had made my decision to continue hustling so whoever he decided to deal with was fair game. Olando up graded his security badge for a gun working as a detention officer at the Mecklenburg county jail. Olando and I lost contact for a few year's when I saw him again he was married with a child.

I heard from God

I heard from God and this is what he said I know you're not the one they thought I'd choose. I know you're not the one they thought I'd use but I choose you.

I know you had a lot trouble in your past I know you cursed people out when they made you mad, but I choose you.

I know your credits not good and you live in the Hood, but I choose you. I heard from God and this is what he said. I know you don't have many friends and you slept with a lot of men but in the end, I choose you.

I know you didn't finish school and sometimes you act a fool, but I choose you. I heard from God and this is what he said I know you were the plug and you sold a lot of drugs, but I choose you.

I know you stayed up a lot of nights couldn't seem to get it right, but I choose you. I know you didn't always do what I said when I said it you were kind of hard headed, but I choose you. I heard from God and this is what he said.

Doors I open no one can close and when I'm done I hope everybody knows that you're my daughter and your beautifully woven, you're my child and you were chosen.

I know your tired your life hasn't been a walk in the park but you're a master piece I created you in the dark.

CHAPTER 9

I didn't worry about the police that much in the beginning or the robbers. I didn't worry about the robbers because the one's that everybody else feared I knew. They knew I didn't get down with that robbing shit. It wasn't that I couldn't be touched hell anybody could be touched. I was just a different kind of drug dealer.

I wasn't trying to make a name for myself. I had nothing to prove to anybody and I had nothing to lose. I know I took the projects by storm. Most people sale drug's in the project's where they grew up at. I never did. I moved to South Side projects and set up shop. I made just as much money if not more than some of the dudes that lived there all their lives.

It wasn't hard to do. The dudes in the hood was too worried about the next dude making more money than them. They didn't even realize that I was sitting on a gold mine at 401 Benjamin. Not only was my location good my attitude was good, and I was extremely humble.

I know your probably wondering how can a drug dealer be humble? I don't know, you would have to ask God. Growing up I was taught respect. I was taught to always respect yourself, and to have respect for your fellow man.

I learned on my own how to respect the game. Some of the dudes in the hood not just the ones from South Side either. They talked to the user's as if they were beneath them. They acted as if they were better because they sold drug's and didn't do them. I couldn't help but think to myself where did some of these ignorant dudes come from?

I had been living in South Side for about a year and a half when my home girl Dee moved there. I knew Dee from BHP she was dating my friend Anne's brother Pud. I was already getting plenty of money and with Dee moving there for her it would be no different.

By me and Dee being female hustlers in what was a man's world would put plenty of talk in the mouths of haters. I can recall my people having a drought. So, against my better judgement I did business with someone that had it, but they didn't have a hell of a lot of it. I would just purchase a few ounces here or there and I would ask is the weight good.

Hell yeah, the weight good is what he would say in return. I tell you Men think they have all the sense in the world. I guess he thought I wasn't going to weigh the shit and take his word for it. He always shorted me every time I dealt with him and I didn't say a word.

I had made up in my mind I was going to wait on my people to get straight. Then a couple days later he brought his backwards hustling ass over my house. He said if you buy five I will front you five. I told him ok.

A couple of days later Dee was at my house. We called the dude up and told him that the police had ran in my spot and what all we didn't flush I swallowed. He started to panic on the phone saying drink milk, drink milk. When he got to my house I was sitting on the couch drinking a glass of ice cold Pet milk.

The next weekend Me and Zandra went to Atlanta and had a ball. That was my first and only time doing that. I can't see how he thought he was going to keep screwing me and not get screwed. When me and Zandra wasn't in the city we were in Atlanta hanging out at 112 and Atlanta Live.

Atlanta was an escape for us. It was a place where nobody knew us, and they could have cared less about our reason's for being there. When we went to Atlanta we left the drugs and the life style behind in Charlotte, but of course we brought the money.

Zandra liked to shop I did also but more so for my kids than myself. I've never been the type of person to care about what others thought of me. Whatever their opinion of me were just that their opinion.

By Zandra being out going and out spoken she didn't meet any strangers. Myself on the other hand had this look about me that automatically told dudes to stay away. Men that saw me would say smile it's going to be alright. Nothing was even wrong. I was very happy in the inside buy you couldn't tell it from my facial appearance.

Once again, my cousin Zandra met a Jamaican named Ken and at the time Zandra didn't care for Jamaican men like that but she talked to him. Ken had a friend named Tray she wanted me to meet. Tray was a fine chocolate Rasta with long dreads. The icing on the cake was they was drug dealers. I don't know if I had a sign on my forehead that said drug dealers only or what.

Zandra would always joke around saying why is it we always ended up with the workers and you end up with the bosses? I thought to myself because I'm a Boss Bitch. My encounter with Tray didn't last long because he was married. I don't like dealing with married men I try to stay away from them.

I am kind of selfish when it comes to my so-called man. I want it when I want it and if you are at home with your wife there is nothing you can do for me. There for I need a single man who can not only put in time but also put in work. I didn't do any business with Tray I didn't even let him know I sold drugs.

When I stopped conversating with Tray I stopped talking to guys completely on a personal level for about six to eight months. If they were not talking money I didn't want to hear it. Even though I sold drugs I was very family oriented. They say old habits die very hard. Every morning I would get up and blast my radio listening to my gospel music. I grew up listening to Shirley Caesar and the Mighty Clouds of Joy, and so that's what I did. Even though I wasn't attending church the way I once was I still paid my tithes. Not that God needed my drug money.

It's kind of hard to change someone's mind about who they think you are especially when they think they have you all figured out. When I was younger the only things I really didn't want people to know about me was what my uncle and two of my cousins had done to me. The older I got the less I cared about anything people found out about me or the lies they told about me.

Now when I look back over my life I wish I would have had enough courage to say I'm not ok. Instead of letting people assume that I was. I guess they thought I was ok because I played and laughed a lot, but I want you to know everybody that laughs and plays a lot doesn't mean they laugh to keep from crying.

On our drive from Atlanta heading home Zandra would always find something to joke about and I would laugh like I was losing my mind. Then the thought about what task I had waiting on me back in the city of Charlotte would always put me back in my mental zone. Truth be told I was struggling. Not financially but mentally and spiritually.

I wanted to love some body but more important than that I wanted someone to love me. I was a grown woman with the mind- set of a teenage girl when it came to sex. I was under the impression that the more sex I had with you the deeper in love you would fall in love with me.

Each relationship at some point I thought this is the one I don't have to look any further but as you'll see that wasn't the truth. I am not saying I slept with fifty different men but the way I was raised if you slept with eleven that wasn't your husband it was to many.

In my late twenties I stopped worrying about men and what they wanted or thought. It wasn't that I wasn't interested in men anymore I just put more interest in myself and my kid's. I had to endure being alone while a single mother and find a way to be ok with it.

ENDURE

I'm going to fight this battle endure the pain. I'm going to walk through the fire and run through the rain.

I will be victorious in Jesus name. Lord while I'm doing your will help me to be quiet and stand still.

Lord please cover my face, so people won't see me but see you in my place. I haven't always been saved and some days I do slip, but by the grace of God I'm still equipped to do what he's called me to do which is focus on me and not worry about you.

God doesn't have to remind me that he's the boss, but he does have to remind me to stop complaining and pick up my cross anyone who say's they have it all together their telling a lie because if they did, Jesus wouldn't have had to die.

If we could have saved our self, God wouldn't have sent somebody else not just anybody he sent his son because he was the only one with pure blood that could get the job done. To believe in Jesus cost you nothing not to believe will cost you everything.

CHAPTER 10

Sometimes I would sit on my front porch just to think and clear my mind. I had started seeing a new guy that would walk pass my apartment. For a while he wouldn't say anything and then out the blue he started speaking to me

. He would say what's up with your ugly self. That shit was so funny to me because he and I both knew there wasn't anything ugly about me. I may not have been the finest apple out of the bunch, but I surely wasn't the ugliest.

I watched Melvin around the hood and I figured out he was a trap dude. Melvin had two brothers David and Derrick. Derrick was away in college when Melvin and I met. Melvin was the oldest out of the three and the darkest. Melvin and I hooked up and the sex was good, and he was convenient.

I don't think Melvin or myself expected our sexual encounters would lead to a serious relationship. Melvin hung with a group of guys that he knew from Tuckaseegee, as for myself I didn't need or like a bunch of people around me that could get me locked the hell up.

I didn't know who Melvin connect was and he surely didn't know mine. Melvin and I was good together for a while. We understood one another and unlike Olando he understood the streets and he didn't try to change my hustle.

I know Olando only wanted the best for me. Olando wanted something for me that I didn't know how to get for myself. In return I settled for less and I choose to be with a man who was ok with my life style and who didn't challenge me or my mind to bigger or better thing's.

However, that didn't make Melvin a bad guy it just made him a typical guy. Melvin was the first guy to buy me anything other than food. Melvin bought me a very nice coat for the winter.

Melvin use to drink a lot and hang out half the night with his so call friends. I can recall Melvin and I going bowling one night. We had a ball. While we were at the bowling alley I called my connect to meet me at my apt, so I could re up.

When Melvin and I got into the parking lot I got out of the car and got into the car with my people. Melvin was drunk so instead of him going into the house he came to the car opened the car door and ordered me to get out. I wouldn't so he pulled out a gun and started shooting in the air.

I got out of the car and my people pulled off and we never did business again. When we got into the house Melvin hit me so hard in my face and head that I fell to the floor and I didn't move I didn't even say a word. I played dead, so he wouldn't hit me again.

Melvin panicked he started screaming for David. David came into the room and saw me laying there. While David was cursing out Melvin and they were trying to figure out what they were going to do. I jumped up off the floor and ran down the stairs and out the door.

When Melvin caught up with me he was telling me how sorry he was. That was the first and last time he ever hit me. I had been through a very abusive relationship with Clay and I promised myself that no other man would ever have that much control over me.

Melvin and I continued to date, and I got pregnant. During the beginning of my pregnancy I met Peter and Shay. They were two young Jamaicans that had it. I really liked them, and they really liked me. During that time, I had a new neighbor moving in. Her name was Lisa she was born in California, but she was moving from Florida.

Lisa was very awkward and not use to the projects at all. When Lisa and her daughter Shay was moving in I was throwing Melvin shit out the front door. When Lisa and I started to conversate she said her first impression of me was that I was crazy. Not throw me in a mental hospital crazy but don't fuck with me type of crazy.

Lisa and I became very good friends and Shay and Synaria had gotten so close they started telling people they were cousins. Melvin and I didn't stay mad at one another for long and he was back at the house. I didn't have a routine that I followed but I would go to BHP at least four days out of the week.

One afternoon in BHP I was walking from my aunt Magelene's house who everybody calls Pogal. I was approached by a man named Tim. Tim was the father of two guy's I knew. One of them I was cordial with, and the other I didn't fuck with because he was a robber.

If you don't know anything about street life one thing is certain drug dealers and robbers don't mix very well. Unless you're a shady ass drug dealer. We already know the robbers are shady they don't give a fuck. That includes the one's in my family they are not excluded from what I am saying.

Tim was trying to holler at me and in the nicest way I could put it without being rude was that I was dating someone. Tim wasn't trying to hear what I was saying so I walked off. Later, in the afternoon I went to Ronnie and Larry Lonts house.

Their mother Mrs. Brenda and my aunt Dot were very good friends at the time and we was all like family. Ronnie and Larry had an older brother that I was friends with named Mikeal Long. Mike and I was cool, but he stayed in prison more then he stayed home.

If Mike would have been home the next thing I am about to tell you it wouldn't have ever happened. While I was at their house Tim walked in. I didn't think anything of it, so I stayed another fifteen to twenty minutes.

When I started to leave Tim started calling me stuck up and saying I thought I was too good to talk to him. I tried to brush it off because I thought he was drunk. I ignored him that is until he spit in my face. I was furious, and my feelings was hurt I couldn't understand how a simple statement (I have a boyfriend) could lead to this.

Even though I was mad I wasn't crazy I knew I couldn't beat a man, but I also knew him spitting on me wasn't going to be the end of it. I called Melvin and I was crying and upset. When Melvin figured out what I was saying he said I am on the way.

I left the Long's house and cut through BHP to aunt Pogal's house. It was about fifteen minutes later Melvin pulled up with David, Eli and a couple of other people. Melvin was like where is he and about that time Tim was walking out the house. Melvin walked up to him and said do you know Reecie. Tim said yeah but. Melvin said but hell. Melvin jumped on Tim like white on rice.

When the fight was over Eli said let me piss on the nigga that's worse than spitting on a mother fucker. David wanted to shoot him. I was on the porch praying because even though I was upset about Tim spitting on me I didn't want him shot or killed.

That's not something I wanted on my conscience. We all left and went back to South Side. Later that night I received a call from one of the twin's he said Doe Doe Tim and a couple of his sons talking about coming to your house. Melvin was in the background saying let them come they won't leave out this bitch. To make a long story short they never came. I continued to go to BHP and no one said a word about what had happened except my family.

I was about three months pregnant and I was in the house all the time and Melvin never was. One of Melvin's friends came to me and said Reecie Melvin cheating with a girl in your neighborhood. He told me what street she lived on, but he didn't know the address.

93

I grabbed the biggest knife I could find out of the house. I told Lisa what was going on and we went to look for Melvin. I didn't go up there to confront the girl or Melvin. I went to get my damn car. I took the knife because I was pregnant, and I didn't know how serious it was between Melvin and this woman.

I wasn't going to fight her over Melvin he wasn't even worth it and if you ask me no man is worth going to blows over. When I saw Melvin and his friends and some females I said give me the keys to my damn car.

Melvin said "what's wrong? What's going on baby?" I didn't answer I left his ass standing there with his new found click. Two days later I had an abortion. There was no way in hell I was going to have a child with that inconsiderate bastard.

It was about a week later one of Melvin friends called my phone saying Melvin had been shot. I asked him why the hell was he calling me. I guess I was still mad at the time because everything was still fresh, the cheating and then the abortion.

I put my feelings aside and I went to see Melvin the next day. When Melvin was released from the hospital he needed someone to take care of him and change his bandages, so he came home with me. I had no intentions of ever dating Melvin again. After a couple of weeks my birthday rolled around. One of Melvin friends picked him up and I was concerned about him, so I asked where he was going because he was on crutches.

Melvin said he had to handle some business. Melvin came back and while I was giving him his dinner he asked me to hand him something from under the pillow. When I reached for it, it was a diamond tennis bracelet. The bracelet was nice, but it couldn't undo the hurt and pain Melvin had caused me.

I was faithful to Melvin and for him to do me dirty in my own neighborhood where everybody knew who I was there was no way possible I could date him again. If my baby was gone so was his ass. Melvin and I was on speaking terms so when he got messed up with the Feds he called me, and I went to see him at the county jail.

Melvin so called friends had screwed him and a bondsman by the name of RJ. Melvin told me that the feds had a picture of me sitting on my front porch. We all know if the Feds are watching they have more than one picture and people running their mouth.

Melvin said they questioned him about me and he told them I was just his girl. Melvin said the Feds told him she's more than that. Her name has been brought up more than a few times. Melvin told me RJ wrote a statement on me that shit was funny to me because he didn't know shit about me.

I had only met with RJ a few times to pay money on Melvin's bond nothing more nothing less. Keep in mind I hadn't had any run ins with the police at all. I didn't have a record and I wasn't a flashy show off type of drug dealer.

In fact, if you ever saw me or were in my presence you wouldn't think in a million years I was a drug dealer. Melvin being locked up didn't stop me from making my money. One thing I didn't do was sell to any and everybody. All money ain't good money. I learned that the hard way.

With by Lisa being right next door I would call her over and she would take the money out of my house everything except the one's because I wanted to make sure I didn't have marked money. With the big bill's I would send them to the neighborhood store to be bust down.

Every time Lisa left with the money she looked like she was doing something she didn't have any business doing with Melvin being gone Lisa and I became even closer. I talked to Lisa about the emptiness I had inside about the guilt from the abortion from Melvin's cheating. I felt like a lost woman. I felt played and disrespected by not only my lover but my friend.

Words of a Woman Lost

These words are the words of a woman lost and these tears are the tears of a woman who has paid the cost.

Boy I am tired of running around in these streets trying to figure out how we gone eat.

When I am supposed to have a man by my side, but your too busy cheating and telling lies.

I thought I was made for you and you were made for me now my eyes are opened, and I can see.

I should have listened when they said leave you alone instead I tried to convince me, I was right, and they were wrong.

Everybody could see it except me how you beat on my heart and played it like a string.

I thought you love me, and one day you'd take my hand boy the only thing you've done was made it hard for another man.

You took me to meet your mama and I can't understand how such a good woman can raise a trifling ass man.

I asked if you wanted someone to treat your daughter this way you didn't answer the question, but it's written on your face you don't want your daughter with a man with a going nowhere pace.

So, what makes you think that I should settle? I know I can do and deserve better.

I'm tired of these women calling my phone. I can't even go to church and leave you alone.

In your defense you said you never brought them to the house. Is it supposed to make me feel better that you said you didn't give them money and didn't take them out?

That you fucked them at their crib and not my house now that the shit has hit the fan your trying to tell me you can be a better man.

You think that I should forgive you and we go on with our life, but I am not mother Teresa and I am not your wife.

You said I had ways like your mama and she never left you. Well I am not your mama and you can get to stepping.

This is a means to an end and no we can't consider being friends. Before I let you waste anymore of my time I'll take a few shots to the head and I'll be fine.

I won't miss live poetry readings and long walks in the park, I won't miss laying on your chest and talking after dark.

These are things I won't miss because those are things we never did, so I won't cry over spilled milk, but I am about to cry over my spilled Ciroc.

You think I am crazy for calling it quits, because I don't have time for your bullshit. If you would have taken the time to know me then you would have known I don't play childish games nigga I am grown.

There's an old saying play pussy get fucked well I don't have a penis but playing with my feeling's will get you fucked up.

This is not bye for now it's bye for good don't ever contact me again, I wish that you would.

War Wounds

I have war wounds and they run deep. There the kind that won't let me

sleep.

I have war wounds their hard to hide, the kind that pierce my side.

I have war wounds their ten feet tall, there a reminder to stumble but not to

fall.

I have war wounds embedded in my head. There the kind that make me wish

I was dead.

I have war wounds that cut like a knife. There the kind that make me

question my life.

I have war wounds they don't show on my face. If I try to remove one

another takes its place.

I'll have war wounds till the day I die. I don't even bother to ask God why.

Why ask God when I can ask myself, I should have asked God when I

needed his help.

CHAPTER 11

While Melvin was in the county jail he was still in contact with the female he cheated on me with and that was cool because we weren't together anymore. I continued to get money with Peter and Shay. My friend girl Michell introduced me to a guy known as C12 he was one of the members of a dance group called Beta Phi.

I guess you can say at first Contrel was a rebound for me. Guess what I got pregnant again just months after my abortion with Melvin's baby. I was so disappointed in myself I didn't know what the hell to do. It wasn't like C12 and I had been in this long relationship. We had only been seeing each other for a few months.

I made the decisions to keep the baby there was no way I was getting another abortion. Even though I was selling a lot of drugs I couldn't save any money. Selling drugs was never away for me to get rich. I just wanted to be able to provide for my kids and my other family member's.

I never had a for sure plan how all this would end. However, I did know that everything comes to an end and this was no different. One day this guy I knew from BHP came to me. He needed me to hook him up with my connect. I told him no at first because he used to be a known robber. He was the cousin to one of my childhood friends.

He assured me that he wasn't on that type of shit anymore. Besides he was making moves in the city. So, against my better judgement I hooked him up with Peter and Shay. To make a long story short he got in good with Peter and Shay then he robbed them. To add insult to injury he had some crackheads walking around my house with walkie talkies as a look out. Not only did he fuck up my connect he could have gotten me and my kids killed.

I called him to see what was up and he told me not to worry about Peter and Shay they were not going to do anything to me. That wasn't the damn point. They still wanted to do business, but I was kind of scared because I didn't know if it was a plot, so they could kill me for hooking them up with Larry robbing ass.

That was a hard lesson learned. Peter contacted me again and this time Peter and Shay came and brought more cocaine then I have ever seen, and I have seen a lot. I was eight and a half months pregnant with my last child. Peter dumped the cocaine onto the bed and I said I don't want it. Peter said you don't want it I said NO.

Peter and Shay left and the next day I got busted. The first face that I saw was my old neighbor officer Keith Way. Keith was very surprised to see me, and he looked as if he was praying Lord don't let it be anything in this apartment. They searched, and they searched and didn't find any cocaine. However, I did receive a citation for a half of joint that C12, aunt Mae, and Chill Will were smoking.

I lost my apartment behind the citation for the weed. While the vice officers were there I thought about my prayer. Lord if I ever get scared doing this it would be time to quit. When Peter put all that cocaine on the bed I got scared and that was my que to quit. It was like God was saying just like Hell, jail wasn't meant for you.

I was able to get out the game without going to prison, without getting robbed, without snitching. There's not one person who can say my signature is on their motion of discovery. If someone says differently their liars. I had a few weeks before I had to be out of my apartment so one day I walked to the hood store and I made a pit stop at the restaurant that was connected to it.

The restaurant was owned by a middle aged nice looking black man. I had been in the restaurant plenty of times but this day he wanted to hold a conversation with me. He said I heard about you. I hear you make a lot of money over here. I guess what he didn't hear was that I just got busted.

He said I want to do some business with you. He asked me how would I feel about selling Boy? I said what the hell is Boy. He said Heroin. I said I don't know shit about Heroin and I didn't want to know anything about it.

I was trying to figure out why this grown ass Black Man Entrepreneur was trying to get me a young black single mother who was living in the projects to sale some shit that could get me a hundred years. That was my last time in his restaurant. I had made up my mind to go to the salvation army women's shelter because I didn't want to live with any of my family member's.

A couple of days before I left South Side my friend Demetria (Dee) introduced me to her cousin Masheba Withers but everybody calls her Sheba. She said why don't you come and stay with me and my sons at least until you have your baby. I decided to take Sheba up on her offer seeing that I only had two or three weeks before I had my baby.

Shantavia was staying with my mom and my little sister so Synaria and I went to Sheba's. Sheba and I got along extremely well and that was strange to me. The reason it was strange, is because Sheba is mean as hell and she's not a people person. It takes a lot to get close to Sheba but once she considers you to be ok she lets her guards down a little bit. Sheba and Dee's family are my family now and my family is theirs.

With any friendship there's going to be some up's and down's but what holds a friendship together is when each one allows the other to be themselves, to applaud them when they are doing good and not to abandon them when they are doing bad. To be the friend that listens to their stories even though you've heard them a thousand times. To be there for them when family is gone and all you have left is time.

Even though everything was going good at Sheba's I didn't stay for long. I didn't want to get comfortable in someone else's home because I had gotten use to my own place. I packed up my belonging's and Synaria and I went to stay at the Salvation Army Women's Shelter. While I was there I meet Derhonda and Barbara Green. They helped me get situated into the shelter.

I went into labor while living at the shelter. I had another daughter on June 25, 1998 who I named Aveonda. Even though I went back to the shelter I didn't take Aveonda with me. Her immune system wasn't strong enough and I didn't want her to get sick. Aveonda stayed with her dad at his mom's house in South Side.

Every day I would leave the shelter at 7am to go spend time with my baby. It took a lot out of me being away from my newborn daughter, but I found peace in knowing she was with the one person who loved her just as much as I did. I also knew that my situation wouldn't last for much longer. What ended me and C12's relationship was the fact that he slept with one of my so-called friends while I was living at the shelter and then wanted to jump on me for calling it quits.

What C12 didn't know was that I learned a long time ago if a man beats on you one time he will do it again if given the chance. They say where there's smoke there's fire. If you're in a relationship and you see smoke, get out of it before you burn. If your anything like me when I was younger, and my mom tried to tell me about things to avoid and thing's she saw coming before they happened. I would say mom I have to live my own life and make my own mistakes you can't prevent every bad thing that's going to take place.

If I would have known the voice that spoke words of wisdom, then it would have saved me from unnecessary grief and pain I could barely endure. With my mom being born in York, South Carolina with my grandparents and my aunts and uncles I didn't realize that depth of her being and what made her who she was.

Now that I sit back and reflect on my life I wish I would have listened to the voices of reason. The voices of women who picked cotton as children until their fingers would bleed. If only I had listened to the voices of my father James and my uncle Ted who went across country prepared to fight a war that they would never see, then maybe just maybe there wouldn't be a reason for this book.

While I was at the shelter I found out about a program for women with addictions. I had an addiction to sex, but I didn't think that was on the list for housing. I lied and told them that I was addicted to weed and to make the lie legit I smoked some just to have it in my system if they tested me. They say desperate times call for desperate measure's and it had proven so in my life.

Don't think it's crazy that I would lie to put a roof over my children's head. Hell, you're talking about a woman who sold cocaine to take care of them. I'm not proud of all the things that I've done and it's like a battle going on in my mind. I am trying to figure out how I can still love my uncle so much and choose to see the good in him and not the bad deeds from his youth.

I struggle trying to find the beauty in all my ashes. It's a battle everyday with people who think they know me. They say you're a sweet girl you have a good heart your cute and oh yeah God has a calling on your life you were chosen from your mother's womb. I listen to them talk and I would say to myself I am unclean, I am unworthy, and what could God possibly have for me to do. I felt ugly not from the outside in but from the inside out. I had committed every sin just about and if I didn't do it, oh best believe I thought about it. Thinking about it is just as bad. There was a battle field going on in my mind and I was my own worst enemy.

Battle

How can beauty and hate be wrapped in the same skin?
In this brown body that I battle with in.

Through dark brown eye's I see nothing but gloom before I came out my mother's womb they said I was doomed.

They say life and death is in the tongue so over my life they spoke death poverty and bad health now I must speak life back over myself.

With thick brown thigh's men seem to like but when I look in the mirror I say I'm alright

Beautifully and wonderfully made by God but with my intellect it seems kind of hard.

To believe or even value my worth when I am living in hell on earth.

With so much pain it cut's like a knife because majority of my life I've seen misery and strife.

Molested by an uncle raped by a familiar face tear's flowing voice unheard now do you understand why I'm kind of disturbed.

So once again I ask you how can beauty and hate be wrapped in the same skin? In this brown body that I battle within.

They spoke low self-esteem, self- pity, confusion, crazy, lazy, no motivation, sex slave to Satin.

All these things I started to believe about myself until I realized these maggots were like cigarettes bad for my health.

I had to let go of friends I had for years because the Devil used them to speak to me in my ears.

The battle that's been going on in my mind will come to an end if given some time.

CHAPTER 12

Life After the Trap

When I moved to Davis Lake in 1999 I had no idea what my future had in store for me. I found myself on the north side of Charlotte with no friends and no family. It wasn't that my family had abandoned me. They were just on opposite sides of town. That left me alone with my kids and my thoughts.

My mind went back to my Grandma Ella one of the strongest women I have ever known. She would say anything worth having is worth working for. They say that the man is the head of the house but not only was my grandma the head of the house she was the head of the entire family in my eyes.

Growing up I knew my mom loved me even though she never said it. My mom wasn't as good of a parent to me then she was my sister. It wasn't that she didn't want to be she just didn't know how to be. I guess my mom decided that the mistakes she made with me she wasn't going to make with my sister. I had family members say she treats your sister better then she treats you.

Even though I felt like that sometimes I let it go in one ear and out the other. Besides my sister needed her more than I did at that time. I was head strong, and I had put up a wall that was very hard for anybody to break through. I put my time and energy into raising my daughters with the help of my mom, and by providing for them at the time the only way I knew how.

Thinking back to what my grandmother said. I realized I had nothing because I didn't really work for anything. Yes, I sold drugs and I made plenty of money but the faster I made it the faster I spent it or gave it away. I didn't have anything on my side but time. Time to reflect on my twenty- eight years of living, and time to figure what to do with the remaining time I had left.

I thought about the men in my life that I once loved and the ones who said they loved me. In that moment I realized I never truly loved any of them. I had genuine feelings for them, but I hadn't ever been in love with anybody.

When it came to love I was damned if I did and damned if I didn't. If I would have allowed someone to infiltrate the wall that other people built around me and the wall I allowed to stay. I was setting myself up for failure.

If I would have opened my heart and let my guards down and give a man my all. Then he would have the power to break my heart and break me down and I wasn't sure how much I could take. I found out that I was cheating myself of allowing someone to love me and learning myself to love someone in return.

The one thing that majority of people in life wanted which was to love and be loved. I feared. I had been living in Davis Lake for a couple of month's when my friend Michell contacted me. And around the same time Trivia had found out where I was located at also. They both came to visit for a few weeks. All of us was single except Michell. She was separated from her husband and by the looks of it that marriage was over.

During that time, we didn't sit around and bash men however we did have plenty of drinks. We discussed the mistakes we had made and talked about our lives as single parent's and how we were going to handle all the pressure.

It was more pressure on Michell because she was using to taking care of her kids in a two- parent home but now she was alone. Myself on the other hand had always been a single parent. That didn't mean I had less stress. It was that I had always been a single mother. The pressure Michell was just beginning to face. I had always faced it.

My heart went out to her because being a single mother or father was no walk in the park. Trivia had troubles of her own. Not only was she a single mother, but her kids were not always in her custody.

She had a drug problem with cocaine that I recently found out about. Trivia never came to me for cocaine. I don't know if she thought that I would look at her differently or she just didn't want me to know. Trivia was younger than me and I couldn't help but wonder what led her down her path of drug abuse.

It didn't matter what Trivia did in the street she was a good person with a good heart and I wasn't going to stop being her friend who was damn near like a sister because she did drugs. Besides she didn't stop being my friend because I sold the shit. She wasn't any better than I was, and I surely wasn't better than her. In the eyes of God, we both were wrong.

Trivia had an addiction to drugs and men and I had an addiction to money, sex and bad boys. When Trivia knew that I found out about her doing cocaine she didn't come around as much as she used to. When she did come around she was never high. I have never seen her like that.

Tyvonne, Talvi and Fatma were pretty good during that time even though they had struggles of their own. Their father Tyrone who we call Cut was ex-military like my father. Uncle Cut's mother's name was Mrs. Irene. I had a lot of respect for Mrs. Irene. I remember being at the Charlotte transit when I was a round eighteen or nineteen years old.

The weather was bad and there was ice on the ground. I saw Mrs. Irene trying to hurry up and catch a bus to work. She fell twice on the ice before I could get to her. When she fell the third time I was right there but still not close enough to catch her.

When I helped her up tears were streaming down my face. I was hurt and amazed at the same time. I was hurt because she nearly broke her neck trying to get to a dead-end job that didn't pay her enough to buy a house to get out the projects. I was amazed at her endurance, her determination to still catch a bus to work. Mrs. Irene was in her mid to late fifties at the time.

I didn't know why God allowed me to be around to see and hear the things that I did because it stayed on my mind heavy. I didn't know then, but I know now. I was going to be the one to tell the stories they couldn't tell. Thinking back on Mrs. Irene I now know for myself how it felt to fall and want to stay down but have the determination to get back up because there's something required of me from God.

One day Trivia, Michell and myself was at my apartment playing around with the kids. My phone started to ring it was my little cousin Fatma. Fatma was calling me about a guy name Willie. John, whom is a childhood friend had brought him to BHP. Fatma was fast for her age and she thought Will was fine as wine.

She also knew he was too damn old for her she was only fourteen. Will was twenty-one at the time. Fatma said cuz it's a guy over here I want you to meet I think you'll like him. She put Will on the phone and I gave him my address.

I wasn't looking for a boyfriend, but he was someone who could come lay and keep me company. When Will knocked on the door and I opened it my jaw dropped. The brother was over six feet tall and fine as hell. He was lighter than I preferred because I had a thing for dark skinned brothers.

I was able to look past that small issue. Will started coming over almost every day and it wasn't just to see me. Will loved kids and he had a daughter of his own. Will and my daughters got along great and he treated them like his own. Will and I started dating and I slowly but surely let my guards down and he started to tear down the wall that had been up for years.

Will and I had gotten extremely serious, but I wouldn't allow my kids to call him Dad. They had fathers even if they were not around. Will was looking for a career change, so he started talking about joining the Navy. Even though I loved Will I didn't want to stand in his way of pursuing his dreams.

Will ended up joining the Navy and asking me to marry him. My answer was yes, and I missed him terribly during his basic training. The one thing that I didn't consider and that would be a deal breaker was that Will wanted more kids and I didn't. I had my kids at a young age and raised them alone. With all I went and had my tubes tied.

I didn't think long term I only thought about the here and now. When I had my last child, never in my wildest dreams did I imagine someone would want to marry me. I had three young children with three different fathers.

Will came home from deployment and we went to get the marriage license. One night before it was time for Will to leave we began to argue in the car. I honestly don't remember why. When the car stopped Will jumped out and that was the beginning to the end of our relationship.

I never cried so much in my life. I pleaded with God and tried negotiating with him. God, I said if you bring him back I will do this and will do that. How many of you know there's no negotiating with God? The bottom line was Will wasn't for me.

To tell you the truth I don't think either one of us was ready for marriage. We were more caught up in the idea of marriage. I gave Will more of my time then I gave God and God is a jealous God and he won't have anyone before him. Unknowingly I put Will before God.

The God who woke me up every morning the God that made sure me and my kids had clothes and food. The God that kept me in my right mind who gave me sight and the ability to use all my limbs. The same God that healed my heart after Will was gone. Will would call from time to time to check on me and the kids and suddenly, the calls stopped.

By that time, it didn't matter because I was over him. Will was the first man I was in love with and I thought he was the last. I don't have any regrets about falling in love with Will the only regret that I have now is that I haven't allowed myself to fall in love again.

If I ever fall in love again I will let God choose the man. Will contacted Synaria on Facebook a few months ago and she gave him my number. We caught up on old times and he told me he had 10 children.

I said Thank You God you always know what is best for me. There is no way in hell I would have had all those children. God gave Will his heart's desire children and lots of them. I'm happy for him. When will and I separated I moved closer into town. I started looking for a job, so I could take care of my children legally.

I applied at Mecklenburg County Park and Recreation. I was interviewed by Paul Roger's the supervisor at the time. Paul asked me are you sure you want to do this job there is only one other women who worked in that department. I assured him that I could and would do the job.

Paul decided to give me a chance and he wasn't disappointed. Paul knew that I was a single mother and he also knew that even though I did my job my mind was on my children especially Aveonda because she was only four. I hated leaving my children even though they were with people I knew, I still couldn't afford child care.

I didn't want my children being molested or mistreated so I kept a close eye on them and the people I allowed around them. My baby sitter didn't show up one day, so I called my cousin John and him along with my cousin Buster came to watch Ave.

I had a puppy at the time and Ave played with him all the time. John called my phone while I was leaving work. John said this damn dog has Diarrhea, and he shitted all over Ave. When I walked into the house John had Ave and the puppy in the tub. I died laughing.

Things are supposed to get better when you get a job but for me it seemed the opposite. They cut off my food stamps because I made six dollars too much. They cut off my Medicaid. They cut mine, but not the kids. The kids continued to get there Medicaid so that was a good thing.

My rent went up and I wasn't making but nine dollars an hour. I had to go back to the only other thing I knew, and that was selling drugs. I kept my job and I hustled on the side just to keep food in the house and to pay rent and my high ass utility bills.

Paul would tell me I haven't seen a woman work as hard as you and care so much for their kids. He said that because most young women he knew wanted to party all the time and leave their children on other people.

When I was growing up God would deal with me in my dreams and visions. One day when I got off work I went to Aunt Mag's house in BHP. While I was there I saw John. We were both headed in different directions and for some reason I told him not to go and get himself in any trouble.

John told me not to put any bad mouth on him. I told him I wouldn't do anything like that. We both knew trouble is easy to get into and hard to get out of. We both said we love one another and departed our way. The next day I heard that my Aunt Katherine was looking for John because she hadn't heard from him. Even though my aunt was on drugs at the time she loved her sons.

I don't know if she felt like something was wrong, but she knew it was out of character for him not to get in touch with her. That following night I had a dream that John had been shot in the head and he was in a wooded area. I jumped up and called my mom because the dream seemed so real.

My mom said Reecie your supposed to take your dreams backwards if you dream about a man it's really a woman. I said ma it was him I could see his face just as clear as day. That evening on the news they reported finding a body in Lincolnton but there was no ID on him.

A few of my family members went to Lincolnton and they had fliers made up. They were going to post the fliers to see if anyone knew who he was. When I saw the flier, my cousin was laying in the woods he looked like he was sleeping. It just so happened a developer was surveying the land and found him.

John's death was extremely hard on our family, but they did arrest the ones responsible, but I don't think they got everybody who planed it. I could be wrong though. I told Paul that I wouldn't be able to work at the county anymore because I didn't have child care. Paul had me fill out a hardship form and I left the county in the proper way, so I could work there again if I needed to.

John's death turned my aunt Katherine's life all the way around. She got saved, she got clean and she's been serving God ever since then. That happened in 2000. Being in the projects for me just wasn't the same. I already had trust issues I really started looking at people differently especially the guys.

When they would come up to me giving their condolences. I couldn't help but to wonder if they had prior knowledge of the murder. When John died I was angry, not at God but at the whole situation. It was about time for his father to come home from prison and he always talked a lot about what he and his father was going to do.

It was always positive things. I am just sad they didn't get to do it. I heard a few different versions about why the murder took place. The first story I heard was they went on a lick. For those who may read this and don't know what lick mean's it's a robbery. They said the person or people he went with got greedy and wanted to keep all the money. They also said my cousin John wasn't going for it, so they shot him in the back of his head.

The craziest thing I heard was that my cousin Buster had got into something. They said when the people caught up to Buster he said it wasn't him it was John. That story broke my cousin Buster down. Buster and I had a conversation a few days after the murder. Buster was crying because he overheard my aunt say I wish it would have been Buster instead of John.

Now keep in mind we were all first cousins. We are sisters and brother's kids. Everybody was torn up behind John's murder. One thing about me I am very observant I had to be. I learned that early on trying to be one step ahead of a pedophile. Once I started selling drugs I had to be on extra alert for the police.

The day of John's funeral after everybody had viewed the body, my cousin Buster walked in. He fell to his knees before he could even make it to the casket. Granted all of us were hurting as well as Buster. Buster seemed to have a different type of hurt. The kind of hurt that pierce's you're very being like a rape. Not only did he have to deal with never seeing John again. He also had to deal with the fact that the streets were talking and even some of the family.

Everybody was blaming him for John being dead. We were used to the street's talking because that's what the streets do. To have your family talking against you that's a different type of betrayal especially if it's lies.

It is one thing to think the shit but to start treating people differently because of what you heard was crazy to me. That's exactly what some of my family members did to my cousin Buster. People thought John and Buster was like night and day but in all actuality, they were more alike than different.

The only difference was Buster started hustling. That's not surprising because Buster and Bigum was basically born into the game. I guess Buster was trying to make money the way he had seen his father. They say the apple doesn't fall far from the tree. That's just an old saying but isn't necessarily true.

When I fell out the tree I didn't just land in the yard I rolled out the mother fucker. Even though I had a lot of my mother and father's characteristics more so my fathers, but I did shit my parents wouldn't have ever done. Hustling for Buster didn't start off to well. He was always getting robbed by Rick. I guess Buster got tired of being robbed and started robbing. I had no respect for robbers, for what?

It doesn't take a rocket scientist to be a robber, but it does take guts. Hell, robbing ain't nothing but stealing. Even though I understood why some of them did it that doesn't mean I had to like it. No more than they had to like me selling dope. Before you saw me posted up with some robbers you would have had a better chance of catching me with some drug dealers.

I would have rather been seen with men and women trying to make a dollar not take a dollar. I am not saying I have never stolen anything because I have when I was younger. Stupid shit out of stores here and there lip gloss or maybe gum. I wasn't a known thief. I was a known drug dealer though. I don't condone stealing. The Bible say's thou shalt not steal but if you are going to steal at least still from an establishment that's not going to miss the shit or is heavily insured.

I don't understand for the life of me why people steal from ordinary people who don't already really have shit. Why rob the drug dealers that are risking their life, their freedom, and their family to live this life. I don't know if you missed the memo there is no 401K in this shit. If you don't invest the money and someone takes it when it's gone it's gone and if you are not a true hustler, you'll be back on the bottom with the bottom feeders in no time.

I can tell you right now I don't have any money but what I do have is the knowledge to make some. I made a conscious decision not to continue to go hard. I do just enough to get by and not get caught. My desire to watch my daughters grow up, graduate school, and to start families of their own was way more rewarding then the lifestyle.

Besides it wasn't like I lived a lavished lifestyle and took expensive trips. My money was accounted for I had to take care of family. Family first. The reason I say Buster and John was more alike than different was because Buster did shit everybody knew about and he didn't give a damn. John on the other hand was low key. Even though Buster and John did some of the same shit we didn't find out about it until he was dead.

Then only reason I believed it then was because it came from his closet friends or mine. Some of it they knew about him doing or either they did it with him. John had four friends that I knew about Marcus for sure who they called Fen. Kendall, Tim, and Tony were the names of his other friends. To me anybody else were associates or suspicious. I knew Marcus since he was a child because his Grandmother and my Grandmother was bringing us up in the same church.

I had ties to Marcus before he had ties to John and that made us family. We were not family by blood but by oath. John and Marcus were so close they were like brothers. They were only about seven or eight years younger than me.

From the start we had two things we were familiar with, and that is God and the church. That was before everybody got on drugs and alcohol. When I left the church, I hit the ground running. The church knew, and I knew, that I had left the building what I didn't know was that I was still in the presence of God. When I ran, I ran long, and I ran hard. I had no choice but to look back because my little cousins and sister were behind me.

JOHN

I HAVE A PAIN IN MY CHEST THAT WON'T GO AWAY.

IT'S BEEN THERE SINCE MY COUSIN JOHN WAS MURDERED THAT DREADFUL DAY.

IF I WOULD HAVE KNOWN THAT DAY WOULD BE THE END.

I WOULD HAVE TALKED LONGER TO MY COUSIN MY FRIEND.

WE WERE MOVING TOO FAST. WE WERE DOING TOO MUCH AND ALONG THE WAY WE FELL OUT OF TOUCH.

I SOMETIMES WONDER IF I COULD HAVE JUST SAID GOODBYE WOULD IT KEEP THESE TEARS FROM FILLING UP IN MY EYES.

THINGS LEFT UNSAID ARE ALWAYS THE WORSE.

I KEPT REPEATING I LOVE YOU WHILE RIDING BEHIND THE HEARSE.

WHEN I LOST JOHN, I LOST A PIECE OF ME.

I STARTED SPIRALING OUT OF CONTROL, BUT NO ONE NOTICED BUT ME.

MURDER HAS A WAY OF DOING SOMETHING TO YOUR SOUL.

ITS THE KIND OF HURT THAT TURNS A PERSON COLD.

I WAS SILENT FOR A WHILE AND PEOPLE WOULD ASK ME WAS I READY TO TALK.

HELL, NO I WASNT. HOW COULD I BE WHEN THEY JUST KILLED MY COUSIN. MY LIFE WAS OFF TRACK.

I WISHED I COULD HAVE MADE THEM TAKE THAT BULLET BACK.

I THOUGHT OF A MILLION WAYS TO MAKE THEM SUFFER.

THE ONLY REASON I DIDN'T WAS BECAUSE OF MY MOTHER.

ME IN PRISON WOULDN'T HAVE BEEN GOOD.

I WOULDN'T HAVE BEEN ABLE TO TAKE CARE OF MY KID'S LIKE I SHOULD.

YEARS HAVE PASSED, AND IT SEEMS LIKE THE PAIN SHOULD HAVE WENT AWAY. BUT IT'S STILL HERE AT THIS PRESENT DAY.

THE DARK SIDE OF ME WANTS TO TREAT THESE NIGGAS LIKE LINT.

SHOOTEM IN THE HEAD AND THEN REPENT.

BUT I'M A CHILD OF GOD SO I FOLLOW THE LIGHT AND ONE DAY GOD'S GOING TO MAKE IT ALL ALRIGHT.

POEM BY REECIE

HAPPY BIRTHDAY CUZ REST EASY Jontavan Moore

People

People dislike what they don't understand.

People don't understand because they don't want to listen.

People don't want to listen because they don't want to learn.

People don't want to learn because they don't want to grow

People don't want to grow because their stuck in the past.

People are stuck in the past because they can't see their future.

People can't see their future because their overwhelmed by their present.

People are overwhelmed by their present because they haven't allowed God

to be the sail in their ship.

CHAPTER 13

After John died and everything begin to settle Lisa and Shay came to live with me in North Charlotte. It was nice having Lisa around during that time because she kept me grounded. The Sunday after John's funeral I went to Saint Paul Baptist Church for service. While sitting there listening to the sermon all kind of thoughts came to my mind.

I realized the journey that my cousin John had taken, I to would have to make one day so I joined the church. I went to a few services after that, but I wasn't used to the bigger congregations and I stopped attending. Even though I wasn't attending church my prayer life was on point. I kept that open communication between myself and God.

I hadn't seen or talked to my cousin Zandra in a couple of years and out of the blue she called me. She had run into one of my cousins on my mom's side and they gave her my number. Zandra told me how much she missed me. Little did she know the feeling was mutual.

One thing about my cousin Zandra, she knew I was about my money. If it had anything to do with making money she wasn't going to leave me out of it. The only difference this time is it was legit. She was working for a company called St. Mary's and they offered classes to obtain your CNA license. I was all for it, so I took the class.

Zandra had gotten saved and she invited me to her church under the leadership of Pastor Delores Bruce. I enjoyed the church. It was a small congregation and it was a Pentecostal church and that's what I was brought up in.

Zandra's personality hadn't changed at all. She would crack jokes during service and I would laugh to the point I would have to cover my mouth. Pastor Bruce would say Sister Reecie would you like to share what's so funny? Zandra would whisper in my ear and say don't say nothing Dodey. I would listen and shake my head no to Pastor Bruce.

When I first joined the church, they had an alter call. Pastor Bruce said if anyone doesn't know Jesus and hasn't accepted him as your personal savior please come to the alter so you can get saved. It was an awkward silence as everyone looked around the room.

Zandra looked at me and I turned my head and Pastor Bruce was looking at me. I thought to myself I don't know why the hell their looking at me. I am saved. I have been saved since I was a child. I may have been a backslider, but I was saved.

When I accepted Christ, I knew exactly what I was doing. If she would have said do you need to be delivered from something come to the alter then I would have gone. Saved and delivered are two different things. In my opinion if you've accepted Christ one time and you meant it when you did it your saved. I don't believe you can get re saved unless you didn't believe you were saved to start with.

I don't care if you get saved on a Friday night and Saturday all hell breaks out and you curse somebody out from Amazing grace to how sweet the sound it doesn't mean you are not saved. It means you are not delivered yet from cursing.

One Sunday I was at church and my cousin Zandra was absent. When service was over I was one of the first people out the church. I was waiting on Pastor Bruce to come out. In my mind something told me she was going to fall down the steps.

I tried to position myself, so I could catch her if she did fall. Then I convinced myself that she wouldn't fall. I said to myself God isn't going to let her fall. Sure, enough she came out the church and fell down the steps. I said Pastor Bruce I saw you when you fell. She said "sister Reecie why didn't you catch me?" I was silent, because I didn't have an honest answer for her.

There was another lady there and she said, "Pastor she saw you before you fell."

Pastor Bruce said "Reecie that's why you have to stay in the church to develop your gift." Once again, I got scared. I wasn't scared of God. I was scared and unsure of what God expected me to do with the gifts that he had bestowed upon me.

I started getting more depressed. I didn't know who I could talk to about what I was experiencing. I felt like I was suffocating within myself. I fell back from the church once again. What I didn't know was that the building wasn't the problem. I myself was the church and no matter where I ran to God was going to be there. I felt like God was pulling me one way and the devil another. I felt caged.

Caged Bird

I am like a bird in a cage with so much rage waiting to be free from this body that entangles me.

I want to fly high beyond the sky that I can only see with my human eye and stake my claim to what lies above.

I want to be as pure as a dove with so much love flopping my wing's and forget about the simple things that seem so major in my life.

I want to run as fast as I can with my back to the wind and the sand beneath my feet.

I want to dance to my own beat with no retreat and regards to what other's think and keep a positive mind, so I won't sink into the negative thoughts of my past.

I want to be as calm as the water that runs thru the Nile, lay down my cross and rest for a while.

Until I fulfill my purpose and realize my worth, while I am still here on what we call earth.

I want to stop all this stalling and press my way to a higher calling, because this stagnant state I find myself in must come to an end because it's not beneficial to myself or to God.

I want to see my future without forgetting my past and find a meaningful relationship that somehow will last.

I am trying to run this race as swift as a horse and try my best to remain on course without deviating to the left or the right while remaining in God's sight.

I am trying not to stumble and remain humble while waiting on my number to be called.

I want my hands to be clean and my heart to be purged so I won't get the urge to defile my body and sin against God.

I'm trying my best to pass every test but if I fall it doesn't mean I failed because God always prevails when it comes to the one's that he's called.

I could do nothing good on my own accord any good I do is because of the Lord.

To him and only him I will give all the praise so in these last days I will be raised way beyond the rays of the sun after this story I will have my glory, and I will leave the pain of my past behind.

CHAPTER 14

I had been single for about two years before I had an unexpected encounter. My aunt Pogal called me and asked me to ride with her to see my uncle Carl. When we reached the house uncle Carl introduced us to the people there. When they started speaking I realized they were Jamaican.

One of the Jamaican's whom name was Randall tried to talk to me. He asked for my number, but I pretended that I didn't hear him. I went to my car to get my phone and when I came back in the house there was a fine guy sitting on the steps.

Our eyes locked and I walked on by him, and back into the kitchen. A few minutes later he entered the kitchen and uncle Carl introduced him as Fabulous. I asked him what part of Jamaica he was from and he said Kingston.

Fabulous and I exchanged numbers, and Randall looked at me like I was crazy. What I didn't know was that Fabulous was dating Randall's girlfriend daughter at the time. Fabulous was a sweet talker. He would tell me how pretty I was and how happy he was that we met.

Fabulous stopped dating the female he was with and we started spending a lot more time together. Fabulous would take the kids and I to Veteran's park off Central

Avenue. He taught the girls and myself how to play soccer. Fabulous was very jealous but he didn't show it at first.

Fabulous had a cousin by the name of Omar whom I was quite fond of. We got along great. Fabulous cooked a lot Jamaican food and it was new for me and the kids. The food was good, but Fabulous cooked rice so much that my youngest daughter Aveonda stopped eating rice all together.

Six months into our relationship Fabulous and I were lying in bed and he started to tell me a story. He said when he was coming to America he stopped in Canada. While he was in Canada he told me, he was held in a Canadian prison where he was beaten. It was hard listening to this strong Jamaican man talk about one of the lowest points of his life.

I held him in my arms while I pretended not to see the tears fall from his face. I guess he felt that he told me too much. He looked at me and said, "get in the closet Reecie I'm going to kill you."

My response was "if you are going to kill me you are going to have to do it right here. My mom isn't going to find my body in a closet." Fabulous said hmmm and smiled. My mom couldn't stand Fabulous for some reason, but she loved Omar. twelve months into our relationship Fabulous bought a couple of guys to the house and he never did that before.

When the two men walked in my house I had a bad feeling. They walked through my house like they owned it. They didn't speak to me but when they spoke to Fabulous it was Jamaican. When they left I told Fabulous not to ever invite them back over again. He told me that was fine, and he didn't have a problem with that.

Things were good between Fabulous and myself. We showered a lot together and Fabulous washed my body and caressed me in a way that no other man had. I wasn't stupid I knew Fabulous didn't have a nine to five, but he kept money.

I knew he hustled even though I didn't see him doing it. I had taken a job at a retirement home. I really liked my job. Three months into the job I was getting off work and there were two gentlemen in suit's waiting for me.

Come to find out they were Homicide detectives. They questioned me about Fabulous and Omar. They said that their names came up in a double homicide of two Jamaicans. I told them I didn't know anything about it. When I talked to Fabulous he told me the two guys that came to the house were the victims.

A week later Fabulous and his cousin was arrested. While they were in the Mecklenburg county jail two more detectives came to my house. They started threating me telling me that they would have my kids taking away from me if I didn't help them with their investigation. I was so pissed off.

I said to them "so if I did know anything you would risk me and my kid's lives to solve your case." I was so mad that I told them to get the hell out of my house and not to ever come back. Fabulous and his cousin along with Randall were held down town for a couple of years. They were finally let go for lack of evidence.

Fabulous and Omar weren't killers in my eyes. I couldn't even imagine them doing something like that. I have lived my life long enough to know nothing's ever just black and white. When Fabulous got out of jail he came to my house. We showered together, and he made love to me like he would never see me again. After that nigh he left the city.

I missed all the late-night talks and the showers. I told myself that maybe love wasn't in the cards for me. Maybe I was only supposed to be happy for a moment in time and then alone once again. When Fabulous faded away, he faded away like the sand does when it hits the shore. He left the door to my heart open for it to only fall apart once again.

I will never be the same is embedded in my brain. Each day I pray for rain, so I won't have to leave out my door. I sit and listen as the water hits my window pane while I wait for the pain in my heart to end. I knew it was a sin to depend and put my hope into a man.

I gave him more of me then I gave Yahweh meaning God. Truth be told for a split second he was my God and when I came to my senses I was still senseless. Even though I was created in Yahweh's image I could no longer hear his voice and it left me off course. When I reconnected with God I let my flesh die and my spirit be raised so I would no longer be enslaved in my own mind.

After my name coming up in the double homicide with Fabulous and Omar I moved every year. I didn't feel safe. Even though I had nothing to do with the murders it was just an unsettling feeling. Having your name being known by local police and then the Feds was just not sitting to well with me.

I had already evaded the police on the drugs they thought they would find in my possession in 1998. Here it is less than ten years later they tried to connect me with a double homicide with some more Jamaicans. There was some other major thing's my name was brought up in and some of it isn't even true.

People will tell all kinds of lies on you to get out of their situation. Law enforcement probably thinks that I am public enemy number one but that's far from the truth. From the words of Tupac, I ain't no killer but don't push me. God has protected me from a lot of things and there are things that he allowed me to go through. When I came out of it there would be no doubt that God himself pulled me through.

Jamaican Love

He blew through my life like a cool breeze with the ease of Bob Marley's song. No Woman No Cry, his skin was brown like the sand on a beach with the potential to reach my inner being.

His hair was long and wavy, and his Jamaican accent drove me crazy.

Like Mary J and Wyclef John's someone please call 911, because it must be a crime for what he's done to my heart. His soft lips made me shiver each time he would deliver kisses down my spine.

Someone please pour me a glass of wine because I still can't believe this man was mine.

Was he perfect? NO, was he worth it yes?

Like Etta James I would rather be blind then to see this mind blowing, Rastafarian man walk away from me.

Maybe in another life I could have been his wife.

Like peanut butter is to jelly.

If I had to do time he would be my celly.

If this was a perfect world he would be my man and I would be his girl.

But since my life is rough and rugged I guess I will continue to thug it.

Like the song I Found Love on A Two -Way Street seems to be my destiny. Like Anita Baker I was caught up in the Rapture of Love.

CHAPTER 15

It began to be a struggle for me living my life on the edge and on the dark side when I knew I was a child of God and God produces light. Hustling came easy to me. I guess it was in my blood not on my father's side. My father was true blue. My mom's side of the family was a different story.

The Moore's are what people called them. The Moore side of the family had hard core drug dealers, drug user's, pimp's and the list go on and on. Before I started having kids my cousin's Fruit and Weedy would come to Charlotte from Sharon, South Carolina. I introduced Fruit and Weedy to Shawn and Bo Pete.

They were guys from Little Rock apartments that I knew my cousins could chill with without any expectations. Fruit, Weedy, and myself was very close, but after I found out I was pregnant I didn't go down South that much anymore, and their trips to Charlotte was few. We didn't grow apart because I was pregnant we were just starting new chapters in our lives.

Fruit and Weedy don't know anything about my personal life after age seventeen. They don't know about the different men in my life or about the drugs I sold or even my struggle to live a holy life pleasing and acceptable to God. For my cousin's reading this book will be like reading a memoir of someone they don't know because even though they know me they don't really know me.

By me writing this book and telling these different stories has allowed me to release into the atmosphere what the Devil tried to use to cripple my mind, body and soul with. I heard the spirit of the Lord three years ago say that my life was going to be an open book and that I was the one who was going to tell it. I thought to myself I don't know how that's going to happen. I haven't even read a book since middle school. I surely couldn't be the one to write one. Truth be told I don't even like reading books.

During the time that I was dealing with mental health they determined that I had PTSD from past childhood traumas. So, on top of suffering from severe depression I had to deal with post-traumatic stress disorder. My family had no idea what was going on in my personal life, because to them I was fine.

I functioned normally when I was around them and I still had a since of humor. The problem came in when I was alone. My mind was my worst enemy. Thoughts of my uncle Alberts penis rubbing up and down my clean and untouched vagina flashed in my head. I could still feel the feeling of having to vomit.

I would lay in bed at night and my mind would wander. I thought about school and all the things I didn't learn only to realize that majority of the shit that they taught about my people were lie's any way. Growing up thinking all my ancestors were slaves and so called Black People.

The things that I had been taught up until I dropped out of school in the tenth grade and the true knowledge of myself combined with childhood traumas were like a jigsaw puzzle trying to figure out where the pieces went. The things I wanted to know and talk about weren't the things my family seemed to have cared to discuss.

They talked about more family gatherings and dinners Hell, I was tired of eating chicken and fatback. Just feed me with knowledge. I wanted family history and truth. I asked my father's mother what kind of Indian she was, and she said she had no idea. I asked myself how is that possible. Then It dawned on me that not only did she not know who she was she couldn't possibly begin to tell me who I was.

I wanted to know how she was a Pentecostal preacher and preached out of the Bible every Sunday for over forty years and not know that we are the children of Israel. I asked my grandmother for information to start a family tree. She said don't look any further then me and papa meaning grandpa Harry.

She told me I might not like what I find. I said it couldn't be any worse than what I already knew. I wanted to know about my bloodline and how I was related directly to Jesus. I know that I come from a royal priest hood even though I was living like a peasant.

When I would sleep sometimes at night I would hear a voice saying that I didn't know who I was. I had dreams of wealth and prosperity even though I was living in poverty. I knew God wouldn't show me things that weren't already connected to my family or weren't attainable.

I have some very intelligent family member's and I am not sure if they thought I was slow or didn't want to discuss the past. I feel like you must know about your past to understand your present and to pursue your future. I didn't say dwell in the past but at least know the truth about it.

I've found out later in life that my mom was just who she was and there was no changing her. My mom has never apologized to me. Maybe she doesn't know how to or maybe she feels like she's done nothing wrong. With that being said, it doesn't make my mother a bad person she's just set in her ways.

My mom does a lot of hugging and kissing with my grandkids and I love to see that. However, it's still uncomfortable to me hugging her because it feels forced and I am not use to it at all.

I think about my mom a lot and I try to imagine what she had to go through raising me. The one thing I have noticed is my mom has broken pieces just like me. My mom and I still struggle to put our broken lives back together, but we never give up on one another no matter how impossible it may seem some days. I'll tell my enemies and my friend's that no matter what my mom and I go through I will rock with her till the end.

Black man, black man I wish I could pull back the layers of lies you been told.

If it were in my power I would look into your eyes just to see your soul.

Black man you don't know how intelligent you are.

It's not about how much money you have or even a fast car.

Black man you are the strength of every black woman.

We need you to stand up and stop acting like your common.

Black man you're the apple of our eye.

That's why it hurts us to see you with a woman of a different race when you walk by.

Black man stand up and be proud.

Brothers you're the ones that stand out in a crowd.

Black man with the scars of a thousand generations.

You're the ones who birthed a nation.

Black man who carries the weight of the world on his shoulders.

We need you by our side, so you can continue to mold us.

Not by the laying on of hands.

Just by being a strong black man.

Black man, black man tells me what's the deal.

It seems you would rather accept what's comfortable instead of dealing with what's real.

Black man stands up and take your place.

Its your choice to date who you like, but at least let us enter the race.

For my black brothers

If you would like to read more about my life, please be on the lookout for my second book If Walls could Talk two Reecie's Broken Pieces Betrayal of the Worst Kind.

ABOUT THE AUTHOR

Reecie Gaddy is a forty five-year old native of Charlotte, NC. She is the single mother of three daughters and the grandmother of four Grandsons and two granddaughters. Reecie Gaddy is a free spirit who was once bond by depression, guilt, shame and despair. A woman who's still realizing her worth. A woman with the patience of Job and a mouth like Peter. A woman who heard God's voice and decided to listen instead of being disobedient as she has been so many times before. A woman with a trail of mistakes and a future full of promise. A woman who's determined to be who GOD created her to be and not who people said she was. You can contact her on Facebook at Reecie Gaddy or email her at reccegaddy@gmail.com

56470329R00083

Made in the USA
Columbia, SC
27 April 2019